LIFE IN CHRIST

Register This New Book

Benefits of Registering*

- ✓ FREE **replacements** of lost or damaged books
- ✓ FREE **audiobook** – *Pilgrim's Progress*, audiobook edition
- ✓ FREE information about new titles and other **freebies**

www.anekopress.com/new-book-registration

*See our website for requirements and limitations.

LIFE IN CHRIST

Lessons from Our Lord's
Miracles and Parables

The Miracles of Our Lord
Volume 8

Charles H. Spurgeon

We love hearing from our readers. Please contact us
at www.anekopress.com/questions-comments with
any questions, comments, or suggestions.

Life in Christ, Vol. 8
© 2022 by Aneko Press
All rights reserved.
Revised edition 2022

Please do not reproduce, store in a retrieval system, or transmit in any form or by any means – electronic, mechanical, photocopying, recording, or otherwise, without written permission from the publisher. Please contact us via www.AnekoPress.com for reprint and translation permissions.

Scripture quotations are from The Authorized (King James) Version. Rights in the Authorized Version in the United Kingdom are vested in the Crown. Reproduced by permission of the Crown's patentee, Cambridge University Press.

Cover Design: Natalia Hawthorne
Cover Painting: Matt Philleo
Editors: Ruth Clark and J. Martin

Aneko Press
www.anekopress.com
Aneko Press, Life Sentence Publishing, and our logos are trademarks of
Life Sentence Publishing, Inc.
203 E. Birch Street
P.O. Box 652
Abbotsford, WI 54405

RELIGION / Christian Life / Spiritual Growth

Paperback ISBN: 978-1-62245-824-0
eBook ISBN: 978-1-62245-825-7

10 9 8 7 6 5 4 3 2 1

Available where books are sold

Contents

Ch. 1: The Blind Beggar 1

Ch. 2: The Blind Man's Earnest Cries 15

Ch. 3: Jesus Stops 31

Ch. 4: A Gospel Sermon to Outsiders 49

Ch. 5: The Soul's Crisis 67

Ch. 6: Saving Faith 83

Ch. 7: Compassion for the Multitude 101

Ch. 8: Jesus Knew What He Would Do 119

Ch. 9: The Boy's Loaves in the Lord's Hands 137

Ch. 10: The Miracle of the Loaves 153

Ch. 11: Certain Curious Calculations about Loaves and Fish 171

Charles H. Spurgeon – A Brief Biography 189

Other Similar Titles 193

Chapter 1

The Blind Beggar

Then they came to Jericho. And as He was leaving Jericho with His disciples and a large crowd, a blind beggar named Bartimaeus, the son of Timaeus, was sitting by the road. When he heard that it was Jesus the Nazarene, he began to cry out and say, "Jesus, Son of David, have mercy on me!" Many were sternly telling him to be quiet, but he kept crying out all the more, "Son of David, have mercy on me!" And Jesus stopped and said, "Call him here." So they called the blind man, saying to him, "Take courage, stand up! He is calling for you." Throwing aside his cloak, he jumped up and came to Jesus. And answering him, Jesus said, "What do you want Me to do for you?" And the blind man said to Him, "Rabboni, I want to regain my sight!" And Jesus said to him, "Go; your faith has made you well." Immediately he regained his sight and began following Him on the road. (Mark 10:46-52)

This poor man was tormented by two great evils – blindness and poverty. It is sad enough to be blind, but if a man who is blind is in possession of riches, there are ten thousand comforts which may help to cheer the darkness of his eye and alleviate the sadness of his heart. But to be both blind and poor, these were a combination of the sternest evils. One thinks it scarcely possible to resist the cry of a beggar whom we meet in the street if he is blind. We pity the blind man when he is surrounded with luxury, but when we see a blind man in need, and following the beggar's trade in the frequented streets, we can hardly forego stopping to assist him. This case of Bartimaeus, however, is but a picture of our own selves. We are all by nature blind and poor. It is true that we regard ourselves able enough to see, but this is but one phase of our blindness. Our blindness is of such a kind that it makes us think our vision is perfect, whereas, when we are enlightened by the Holy Spirit, we discover our previous sight to have been blindness indeed. Spiritually, we are blind; we are unable to discern our lost estate, and unable to behold the blackness of sin, or the terrors of the wrath to come. The unrenewed mind is so blind that it does not perceive the all-attractive beauty of Christ. The Sun of Righteousness may arise with healing beneath his wings, but it would be all in vain for those who cannot see his shining. Christ may do many mighty works in their presence, but they do not recognize his glory; we are blind until he has opened our eyes.

But besides being blind we are also by nature poor. Our father Adam spent our birthright and lost our estates. Paradise, the homestead of our race, has become dilapidated, and we are left in the depths of poverty without anything with which we may buy bread for our hungry souls, or clothing for our naked spirits; blindness and poverty are the lot of all men after a spiritual fashion, till Jesus visits them in love. Look around then, you children of God; look around you, and you shall see in this hall many a counterpart of poor blind Bartimaeus sitting by the wayside begging. I hope there be many such who come here, who though they be blind and naked and poor, nevertheless are begging – longing to get something more than they have – not content with their position. With just enough spiritual life and sensitiveness to know their misery, they have come up to this place begging. Oh, that while Jesus passes by this day they may have faith to cry aloud to him for mercy! Oh, may his gracious heart be moved by their thrilling cry, *"Jesus, Son of David, have mercy on me!"* Oh, may he turn and give sight unto such, that they may follow him and go on their way rejoicing!

I shall address myself most particularly to the poor and blind souls today. The poor blind man's faith described in this passage of Scripture is a fit picture of the faith which I pray God you may be enabled to exert to the saving of your souls. We shall notice *the origin of his faith, how his faith perceived its opportunity when Jesus passed by*. We shall *listen to his faith while it cries and begs*. We shall *look upon his faith while it leaps in joyous obedience to the divine call*. And then we shall *hear his faith describing his case*: "Lord, *I want to regain my sight*"; and I trust we shall be enabled to rejoice together with this poor believing man when his sight is restored, as we see him in the beauty of thankfulness and gratitude follow Jesus along the way.

First, then, we shall note the origin of this poor blind man's faith. He had faith, for it was his faith which obtained for him his sight. Now, where did he get it? We are not told in this passage how Bartimaeus came to believe Jesus to be the Messiah, but I think we may very fairly risk a conjecture. It is quite certain that Bartimaeus did not come to believe in Christ from what he saw. Jesus had worked many miracles; many eyes had seen, and many hearts had believed because of what they saw. Bartimaeus also believed, but certainly not as the result of his eyesight, for he was stone-blind. No ray of light had ever burst into his soul; he was shut up in thick darkness and could see nothing. How then was it that he came to believe? It certainly could not have been because he had traveled much through the country, for blind men stay at home; they care not to journey far. There is nothing they can see. However fair the landscape, they cannot drink it in with their eyes; whatever lovely spots others may behold, there are no attractions for their blank survey. They therefore stay at home. And especially a beggar like this, how should he travel? He would be perhaps unknown outside of the city in which his father Timaeus had lived – even Jericho. He could not move the heart of strangers to charity, nor would he be likely to find a guide to conduct him throughout the dreary miles of that land. He would be almost necessarily a poor blind stay-at-home. Then how did he acquire his faith? I think it might be in this fashion. On the nearest bank he could find outside Jericho, he sat begging in the sunlight, for blind men always love to bask in the sun. Though they see nothing, there is a kind of glimmering that penetrates the visual organ, and they rejoice in it. At least they feel the heat of the great orb of day if they see not its light. Well, as he sat there, he would hear the passersby talking of Jesus of Nazareth, and as blind men are usually inquisitive, he would ask them to stay and tell him the story – some tale of what Jesus had done; and they would tell him how he raised the dead, and healed the leper; and he would say, "I wonder if he can give sight to the blind." And one day it came to pass, that he was told Jesus had restored to sight a man who had been born blind. This indeed was the great master story that the world has to tell, for it had never been so known before in Israel that a man who had been born blind would have his eyes opened. I think I see the poor man as he hears the story, he drinks it in, claps his hands, and cries, "Then there is still hope for me. Perhaps the Prophet will pass this way, and if he does, oh, I will cry to him, I will beg him to open my eyes too; for if the worst case has been cured, then surely mine may be." Many and many a day as he sat there, he would call to the passerby again, and would say, "Come tell me the story of the man that was born blind and of Jesus of Nazareth who opened his eyes," and perhaps he would even get tiresome, as blind men are accustomed to. He must hear the story told him a hundred times over, and always would there be a smile on the poor fellow's face when he heard the refreshing narrative. It never could be told too often, for he loved to hear it. To him it was like a cool, refreshing breeze in the heat of a burning sun. "Tell it to me, tell it to me, tell it to me again," says he, "the sweet story of the man that opened the eyes of the blind." And I think that as he sat all alone, and unable to divert his mind with many things, he would always keep his heart fixed on that one narrative, and turn it over, and over, and over again, till in his daydreams he would half think he could see, and sometimes almost imagine that his own eyes were going to be opened too.

Perhaps on one of those occasions, as he was turning this over in his mind, some text of Scripture he had heard in the synagogue occurred to him. He heard that Messiah would come to open the eyes of the blind, and quick in thought, having better eyes within than he had without, he came at once to the conclusion that the man who could open the eyes of the blind was none other than the Messiah; and from that day he was a secret disciple of Jesus. He might have heard him scoffed at, but *he* did not scoff. How could he scoff at one who had opened the eyes of the blind? He might have heard many a passerby reviling Christ and calling him an imposter, but *he* could not join in the reviling. How could he be a deceiver who gave sight to poor blind men? I imagine this would be the cherished dream of his life. And perhaps for the two or three years of the Savior's ministry the one thought of the poor blind man would be, "Jesus of Nazareth opened the eyes of one that was blind." That story which he had heard led him to believe Jesus must be the predicted Messiah.

Now, O you spiritually blind, you spiritually poor, how is it that you have not believed in Christ? You have heard the wondrous deeds which he has done; *faith comes from hearing.* You have understood how one after another has been pardoned and forgiven; you have stood in the house of God and listened to the confession of the repentant one and the joyous shout of the believer, and yet you believe not. You have journeyed up year after year to the sanctuary of God, and you have heard many stories – many a glorious narrative of the pardoning power of Christ – and how is it, O you spiritually blind, that you have never thought on him? Why is it you have not turned this over and over in your minds. "This man receives sinners, and will he not receive me?" How is it that you have not recollected that he who put away the sin of Paul and the seven demons of Mary Magdalene can put away yours also? Surely, if but one story told into the ear of the poor blind man could give him faith, if his faith came but by one hearing, how is it that though you have heard many times that there was no salvation without faith in Christ, and listened to many an earnest appeal, yet you have not believed? Yet it may be that I have among these poor blind men some here today that are simply believing. You have never yet laid hold of faith, but still in the depths of your soul there is a something which says, "Yes, he is able to save me; I know he has power to forgive," and sometimes the voice speaks a little louder, and it cheers your heart with a thought like this: "Go to him, for he will not cast you away; he has never cast out one yet who did venture upon his power and goodness." Well, my dear hearer, if you are in this unfortunate situation, you are happy, and I am a happy man to have the privilege of addressing you – it shall not be long before the faith within you, which has been born by hearing, shall acquire strength enough to exercise itself to gain the blessing. That is the first thing – the origin of the faith of poor blind Bartimaeus, that it doubtless came by hearing.

Now, in the next place, we shall notice his faith in its quickness at grasping the gracious opportunity.

Jesus had been through Jericho, and as he went into the city there was a blind man standing by the way, and Jesus healed *him*. Bartimaeus, however, seems to have resided at the other side of Jericho; therefore, he did not get a blessing till Christ was about to leave it. He is sitting down upon his customary spot by the wayside where some friend has left him, that he might remain there all day and beg, and he hears a great noise and trampling of feet. He wonders what it is, and he asks a passerby, "What is that noise? Why all this tumult?" And the answer is, *Jesus of Nazareth [is] passing by*. That is but small encouragement, yet his faith had now arrived at such a strength that this was quite enough for him, that Jesus of Nazareth was passing by. Unbelief would have said, "He passes by, there is no healing for you; he passes by, there is no hope of mercy; he is about to leave, and he takes no notice of you." Why, if you and I needed encouragement, we would want Christ to stand still; we would need someone to say, "Jesus of Nazareth is standing still and looking for you." Alas, but this poor man's faith was of such a character that it could feed on any dry crust on which our puny little faith would have starved. He was like that poor woman who, when she was repulsed, said, "Truth, Lord, I am but a dog, yet the dogs eat the crumbs which fall from the master's table." He only heard, *Jesus of Nazareth [is] passing by*; but that was enough for him. It was a slim opportunity. He might have reasoned thus with himself: "Jesus is passing by, he is just going out of Jericho; surely he cannot stay now that he is on a journey." No, rather did he argue thus with himself: "If he is going out of Jericho, so much the more reason that I should stop him, for this may be my last chance." And, therefore, what unbelief would argue as a reason for stopping his mouth did but open it even wider. Unbelief might have said, "He is surrounded by a great multitude of people, he cannot get at you. His disciples are round about him too, so he will be so busy in addressing them that he will never regard your feeble cry." "Alas," said he, "so much the greater reason then that I should cry with all my might"; and he makes the very multitude of people become a fresh argument why he should shout aloud, *"Jesus, Son of David, have mercy on me!"* So, however slim the opportunity, yet it encouraged him.

And now my dear friends, we turn to you again. Faith has been in your heart perhaps for many a day, but how foolish have you been; you have not benefited yourself of encouraging opportunities as you might have done. How many times has Christ not only passed by, but has also stopped and knocked at your door and stood in your house? He has wooed and invited you, and yet you would not come. Still trembling and wavering, you dare not exercise the faith you have, and risk the results and come boldly to him. He has stood in your streets, *for so many years,* till the poor blind man's hair would have turned gray with age. He is standing in the street today – today he addresses you and says, "Sinner, come to me and live." Today is mercy freely presented to you; today is the declaration made – *Let the one who wishes take the water of life without cost.* You poor unbelieving heart, will you not, dare you not, take advantage of the encouragement to come to him? Your encouragements are infinitely greater than those of this poor blind man; let them not be lost upon you. Come now, this very moment. Cry aloud to him now; ask him to have mercy upon you, for now he not only passes by, but he also presents himself with outstretched arms, and cries, "Come unto me, and I will give you rest, and life, and salvation."

Such was the encouragement of this man's faith, and I wish that something in what I said might give encouragement to some poor Bartimaeus who is sitting or standing here.

In the third place, having noticed how the faith of the blind man discovered and seized upon this opportunity – the passing by of the gracious Savior – we have to listen to the cry of faith. The poor blind man sitting there is informed that it is Jesus of Nazareth. Without a moment's pause or ado, he is up and begins to cry, *"Son of David, have mercy on me!" "Son of David, have mercy on me!"* But he is in the middle of a fair discourse, and his hearers do not like it that he should be interrupted – "Hold your tongue, blind man. Depart! he cannot attend to you." Yet what does the narrative say about him? *He kept crying out all the more;* not only did he cry out more, but he also cried out *all the more,* "Son of David, have mercy on me!" "Oh," says Peter, "do not interrupt the Master; what are you so noisy for?" *"Son of David, have mercy on me!"* he repeats it again. "Remove him," says one. "He interrupts the whole service; take him away," and so they tried to move him, yet he cries the more vigorously and vehemently, *"Son of David, have mercy on me!" "Son of David, have mercy on me!"* I think we hear his shout. It is not to be imitated; no *artiste* could throw into an utterance such vehemence or such emotion as this man would cast into it – *"Son of David, have mercy on me!"* Every word would tell, every syllable would suggest an argument, and there would be the very strength, and might, and blood, and sinew of that man's life cast into it. He would be like Jacob wrestling with the angel, and every word would be a hand to grasp him that he might not go. *"Son of David, have mercy on me!"*

We have here a picture of the power of faith. In every case, sinner, if you would be saved, your faith must exercise itself in crying. The gate of heaven is to be opened only in one way – by the very earnest use of the knocker of prayer. You cannot have your eyes opened until your mouth is opened. Open your mouth in prayer, and he shall open your eyes to see; so shall you find joy and gladness. Mark you, when a man has faith in the soul and earnestness combined with it, he will pray indeed. Call not those things prayers that you hear read in the churches. Imagine not that those talks are prayers that you hear in our prayer meetings. Prayer is something nobler than all these. That is prayer, when the poor soul in some weighty trouble, fainting and thirsty, lifts up its streaming eyes, and wrings its hands, and beats its bosom, and then cries, *"Son of David, have mercy on me!"* Our cold speeches will never reach the throne of God. It is the burning lava of the soul that has a furnace within – a very volcano of grief and sorrow – it is that burning lava of prayer that finds its way to God. No prayer ever reaches God's heart which does not come from our hearts. Nine out of ten of the prayers which you listen to in our public

> **No prayer ever reaches God's heart which does not come from our hearts.**

services have so little zeal in them that if they obtained a blessing, it would be a miracle of miracles indeed.

Are you now seeking Christ in earnest prayer? Be not afraid of being too earnest or too persevering. Go to Christ this day, agonize and wrestle with him; beg him to have mercy on you, and if he hears you not, go to him again, and again, and again. Seven times a day call upon him, and resolve in your heart that you will never cease from prayer till the Holy Spirit has revealed to your soul the pardon of your sin. When once the Lord brings a man to this resolve, "I will be saved. If I perish, I will still go to the throne of grace and perish only there," that man cannot perish. He is a saved man, and he shall see God's face with joy. The worst of us is that we pray with a little spasmodic earnestness and then we cease. We begin again, and then once more the fervor ceases and we leave off our prayers. If we would get heaven, we must carry it not by one desperate assault, but by a continuous blockade. We must take it with the red-hot shot of fervent prayer. But this must be fired day and night, until at last the city of heaven yields to us. *The kingdom of heaven suffers violence, and violent men take it by force.* Behold the courage of this man. He is hindered by many, but he will not cease to pray. So if the flesh, the devil, and your own hearts should command you to cease your begging, never do so, but all the more cry aloud, *"Son of David, have mercy on me!"*

I must observe here the simplicity of this man's prayer. He did not want a liturgy or a prayer book on this occasion. There was something he needed, and he asked for that. When we have our needs at hand they will usually suggest the proper language. I remember a remark of quaint old Bunyan, speaking of those who make prayers for others. "The apostle Paul said he knew not what to pray for, and yet," says he, "there are many infinitely inferior to the apostle Paul, who can write prayers; who not only know what to pray for, and how to pray, but who know how other people should pray, and not only that, but who know how they ought to pray from the first day of January to the last of December." We cannot dispense with the fresh influence of the Holy Spirit suggesting words in which our needs may be couched; and as to the idea that any form of prayer will ever suit an awakened and enlightened believer, or will ever be fit and proper for the lip of a repentant sinner – I cannot imagine it. This man cried from his heart the words that came first – the simplest which could possibly express his desire – *"Son of David, have mercy on me!"* Go and do likewise, you poor blind sinner, and the Lord will hear you as he did Bartimaeus.

High over the buzz and noise of the multitude and the sound of the trampling of feet is heard a sweet voice which tells of mercy, and of love, and of grace. But louder than that voice is heard a piercing cry – a cry repeated many and many a time – which gathers strength in repetition; and though the throat that utters it be hoarse, yet does the cry grow louder and louder, and stronger still – *"Jesus, Son of David, have mercy on me!"* The Master stops. The sound of misery in earnest to be relieved can never be neglected by him. He looks around; there sits Bartimaeus. The Savior can see him, though he cannot see the Savior. *"Call him here,"* says he. "Let him come to me, that I may have mercy on him." And now, they who had told him to hold his clamor change their tune, and gathering around him they say, *"Take courage, stand up! He is calling for you."* Ah, poor comforters! they would not soothe him when he needed it. What did he care now about all they had to say? The Master had spoken; that was enough, without their meddling assistance. Nevertheless, they cry, *"Stand up! He is calling for you,"* and they lead him, or are about to lead him, to Christ, but he needs no leading. Pushing them aside he hurls back the garment in which he wrapped himself at night – no doubt, a ragged one – and casting that away, the blind man seems as if he really saw at once. The sound guides him, and with a leap, leaving his cloak behind him, waving his hands for utter gladness, there he stands in the presence of him who shall give him sight.

We pause here to observe how eagerly he obeyed the call. The Master had but to speak, to stand still, and command him to be called, and he comes. No pressure is needed. Peter need not pull him by one arm and John by the other. No, he leaps forward, and is glad to come. "He calls me, and shall I stand back?"

And now, how many of you have been called under the sound of the ministry, and yet you have not come. Why is it? Did you think that Christ did not mean it when he said, *"Come to Me, all who are weary and heavy-laden, and I will give you rest"*? Why is it that you still keep on at your labors and are still heavy-laden? Why do you not come? Oh, come! Leap to him who calls you! I pray you cast away the garments of your worldliness, the garment of your sin. Cast away the robe of your self-righteousness, and come, come away. Why is it that I tell you this? Surely if you will not come at the Savior's bidding, you will not come at mine. If your own stern necessities do not make you heed his gracious call, surely nothing I can say can ever move you. O my poor blind brothers and sisters! you who cannot see Christ to be your Savior, you that are full of guilt and fear, he calls you:

> Come ye weary, heavy laden,
> Lost and ruined by the fall.

Come you that have no hope, no righteousness; you outcast, you desponding, you distressed, you lost, you ruined, come! Come today! Whoever will, in your ears today mercy cries, *"Stand up! He is calling for you."* O Savior! call them effectually. Call now; let the Spirit speak. O Spirit of the living God, command the poor prisoner to come, and let him leap to lose his chains. I know that which kept me a long time from the Savior was the idea that he had never called me; and yet when I came to him, I discovered that long before that he had invited me, but I had closed my ear. I thought surely he had invited everyone else to him, but I must be left out, the poorest and the vilest of them all. O sinner, if such be your consciousness, then you are one to whom the invitation is specially addressed. Trust him now, just as you are, with all your sins around you, come to him and ask him to forgive you; plead his blood and merits, and you cannot, shall not, plead in vain.

We proceed towards the conclusion. The man has come to Christ, let us listen to his appeal. Jesus, with loving condescension, takes him by the hand and in order to test him, and so that all the crowd might see that he really knew what he wanted, said to him, *"What do you want Me to do for you?"* How plain the man's confession, not one word too many, and he could not have said it in a word less – *"Rabboni, I want to regain my sight!"* There was no stammering here, no stuttering, and saying, "Lord, I hardly know what to say." He just told it at once – *"Rabboni, I want to regain my sight!"*

Now, if there be someone who has a secret faith in Christ, and who has heard the invitation, let me implore you to go home to your chamber, and there, kneeling by your bedside, by faith picture the Savior saying to you, *"What do you want Me to do for you?"* Fall on your knees, and without hesitation tell him all; tell him you are guilty, and you desire that he pardon you. Confess your sins; keep none of them back. Say, "Lord, I implore you, pardon my drunkenness, my profanity, or whatever it may be that I have been guilty of"; and then still imagine you hear him saying, *"What do you want Me to do for you?"* Tell him, "Lord, I wish to be kept from all these sins in the future. I shall not be content with being pardoned, I want to be renewed." Tell him you have a hard heart, ask him to soften it; tell him you have a blind eye, and you cannot see your interest in Christ. Ask him to open it; confess before him you are full of iniquity and prone to wander; ask him to take your heart and wash it, and then to set it upon things above, and permit it no longer to be fond of the things of earth. Tell it out plainly, make a frank and full confession in his presence; and what if it should happen, my dear hearer, that this very day, while you are in your chamber, Christ should give you the touch of grace, put your sins away, save your soul, and give you the joy to know that you are now a child of God, and now an heir of heaven. Imitate the blind man in the explicitness and straightforwardness of his confession and his request – *"Rabboni, I want to regain my sight!"*

> How cheering the fact that the blind man had no sooner stated his desire than immediately he received his sight.

Once again, how cheering the fact that the blind man had no sooner stated his desire than immediately he received his sight. Oh! how he must have leaped in that moment! What joys must have rushed in upon his spirit! He saw not the men as trees walking, but he received his sight at once; not a glimmer, but a bright, full burst of sunlight fell upon his dark eyeballs. Some persons do not believe in instantaneous conversions; nevertheless, they are facts. Many a man has come into this hall with all his sins around him, and before he has left it he has felt his sins forgiven. He has come here a hardened reprobate, but he has gone away from that day forth to lead a new life, and walk in the fear of God. The fact is, there are many conversions that are gradual;

but regeneration, after all, at least in the part of it called "quickening," must be instantaneous, and justification is given to a man as swiftly as the flash of lightning. We are full of sin one hour, but it is forgiven in an instant; and sins past, present, and to come are cast to the four winds of heaven in less time than the clock takes to beat the death of a second. The blind man saw immediately.

And now what would you imagine this man would do as soon as his eyes were opened? Has he a father, will he not go to see him? Has he a sister, or a brother, will he not long to get to his household? Above all has he a partner of his poor blind existence, will he not seek her out to go and tell her that now he can behold the face of one who has so long loved and wept over him? Will he not now want to go and see the temple, and the glories of it? Does he not now desire to look upon the hills and all their beauties, and behold the sea and its storms and all its wonders? No, there is but one thing that poor blind man now longs for – it is that he may always see the man who has opened his eyes. He *began following Him on the road*. What a beautiful picture this is of a true convert. The moment his sins are forgiven, the one thing he wants to do is serve Christ. His tongue begins to itch to tell somebody else of the mercy he has found. He longs to go off to the next shop and tell some workfellow that his sins are all pardoned. He cannot be content. He thinks he could preach now. Put him in the pulpit, and though there were ten thousand before him, he would not blush to say, *He brought me up out of the pit of destruction, out of the miry clay, and He set my feet upon a rock making my footsteps firm*. All he now asks is, "Lord, I wish to follow you to whatever place you go. Let me never lose your company. Make my communion with you everlasting. Cause my love to increase. May my service be continual, and in this life may I walk with Jesus, and in the world to come all I ask is that I may live with him."

You see the crowd going along now. Who is that man in the midst with a face so joyous? Who is that man who has lost his upper garment? See, he wears the dress of a beggar. Who is he? You would not think there is any poverty about him; for his step is firm and his eye glistens and sparkles. And listen to him; as he goes along, sometimes he is uttering a little hymn or song, or at other times when others are singing, hear his notes, the loudest of them all. Who is this man, always so happy and so full of thankfulness? It is the poor blind Bartimaeus, who once sat by the wayside begging. And do you see yonder man, his brother, and his prototype? Who is it that sings so heartily in the house of God, and who when he is sitting in that house, or walking by the way, is continually humming to himself some strain of praise? Oh! it is that drunkard who has had his sins forgiven; it is that swearer who has had his profanity cleansed out; it is she who was once a harlot, but is now one of the daughters of Jerusalem; it is she who once led others to hell, who now washes her Redeemer's feet and wipes them with the hairs of her head. Oh, may God grant that this story of Bartimaeus may be written over again in your experience, and may you all at last meet where the eternal light of God shall have chased away all blindness, and where the inhabitants shall never say, "I am sick."

Chapter 2

The Blind Man's Earnest Cries

When he heard that it was Jesus the Nazarene, he began to cry out and say, "Jesus, Son of David, have mercy on me!" Many were sternly telling him to be quiet, but he kept crying out all the more, "Son of David, have mercy on me!" (Mark 10:47-48)

Wherever Jesus Christ is found, his presence is marvelously mighty. The disciples, when Christ was absent, were like sheep without a shepherd; they were thwarted in argument, and even defeated in attempted miracles. But as soon as our Savior made his appearance among them, they returned to their usual strength. When a valiant general suddenly hastens to the rescue of his routed troops, the dash of his horsehoofs reassures the trembling, and the sound of his voice transforms each coward into a hero. May the glorious Captain of our salvation show himself in the midst of our churches, and there will be a joyous shout along our ranks. You will have no need to exchange ministers, or to wish for a better class of Christians; the same officers and the same soldiers will suffice to win splendid victories. If Jesus is present, the men will be so changed that you will scarcely know them; they shall be filled with power from on high, and they will do great exploits in his name and by his strength. Nor does the divine energy of his presence confine itself to those who are already disciples of the

Savior; but strangers, neighbors, wanderers, and even blind beggars feel the effect of his nearness. This sightless beggar hears the good news that Jesus of Nazareth is passing by, and right away he begins to pray. My brethren, there shall be no lack of praying hearts where there is a present Savior. If there be no conversions in the congregation, it must be because Christ is not dwelling there by his Spirit. You have grieved him, and he is gone; you have forgotten him, and he has left you, that you may prove your own weakness, and learn to glorify his power in the future. If the Lord shall graciously return to his church, cries of repentant ones will be frequent, and the songs of those who have found peace by faith in him shall go up to heaven in blessed chorus. Oh! that the Lord Jesus would appear among the churches of this our age! We have much to mourn over. Infidelity brashly seats itself in the chief seats of the synagogue. Roman Catholicism secretly eats out the very vitals of our national religion.

Tolerance acts as a moth upon gospel doctrine; inconsistency of life dishonors the profession of practical godliness. O Lord, how long, how long? If the Lord Jesus shall graciously work by his Spirit among us, we shall soon have our languishing churches revived; errors will fly as the bats and owls commit themselves to their hiding places when the sun rises; and every sweet flower of Christian grace shall yield its blessed perfume under the sweet influences of his celestial rays. I thank God we have had Jesus *here*. We have often been able to say, "Jesus is passing by." He is here still. Believing hearts who recognize his presence, and lament when he is absent, tell us that they often find him sweetly manifested to them here in the preaching of the Word, in the breaking of bread, and in the fellowship of prayer. He is here now; but oh! we want to recognize his presence more fully; we want to see the divine influences, like streams from Lebanon, fertilizing all our garden. We desire to see Jesus working more effectually in making poor sinners feel their need of him, and drawing them to himself.

Providence at all times co-works with grace in the salvation of the chosen people. You have an instance of it here. It was providence which brought the blind man where grace brought Jesus Christ. The Lord might have been passing by, but if this blind man had not happened to live at Jericho, or if at that particular moment he had not been pursuing his avocation of begging just on the particular road along which the Savior marched, he would never have heard that Jesus *was passing by*, and consequently would never have cried out to him, and would never have obtained the necessary cure. Providence brings sinners under the hearing of the Word, and moves the preacher to select topics suitable to their minds. Providence prepares them, as the plow prepares the soil, and grace guides the minister's mind to act as the hand which throws the wheat broadcast over the field. I am thankful for many of you that you are here this morning, for I know that "Jesus is passing by"; and though it may be that you are still without the heavenly light, it is a circumstance for which you ought to thank God, that many have *here* received sight from the Lord Jesus. It may be a singular providence which induced you to come here at all – I pray it may prove to be the white horse on which Christ rides forth, conquering and to conquer, that he may win a victory in your souls now.

> Providence brings sinners under the hearing of the Word, and moves the preacher to select topics suitable to their minds.

Permit me, however, to remind you that such a circumstance involves responsibility. Jesus passes by – the blind man sits by the wayside – if he does not cry, his blindness will from that point on be willful; and there will be an addition to all its gloom in the thought that he did not use the one means within his reach, namely, that of crying to the physician for healing. Remember your responsibility, anxious sinner, and ask God to give you grace now to improve the flying hour, and may his Spirit lead you to imitate the example of the blind man, and cry, *"Son of David, have mercy on me!"*

Coming directly to the case before us, let us observe the blind man's earnestness as a contrast with the behavior of many hearers of the Word.

It was a very short sermon that was preached to him. He heard that *Jesus of Nazareth was passing by.* He heard nothing more. I do not know that he understood doctrine, that he precisely knew what Jesus Christ came into the world for. He could not have explained the system of theology. He had never had a clear and distinct statement of grace laid down before him. All he had heard was that *Jesus of Nazareth was passing by.* But that short sermon led him to prayer. Beloved, what a contrast between him and some of you! You have been sermonized until you must nearly be sermon-weary. You have heard the truth till probably, in theory, there are none better instructed than you are. You know the precious doctrines of truth so far as the killing letter is concerned, but you have never yet been led to pray; or, if the prayer has come, it has never been that earnest, heaven-piercing cry which will not be refused: *"Son of David, have mercy on me!"* has not been the passionate prayer of your spirit. How many there are who listen to me so often that I fear I shall never be God's instrument of salvation to them. It is so easy for you to get used to one voice, till that which once was as shrill as the note of a trumpet becomes like the buzzing of a bee in your ears. You weary of it, you sleep under it as a miller sleeps while his mill is going, because it makes no sound to which he is not accustomed. My figures and illustrations you have heard; my tones of pleading you well know; my words of exhortation you can probably repeat by heart; and some of you are no more affected by twelve years of earnest effort than a piece of marble might be affected by twelve years of pouring oil along its hard, unmelting surface.

It is a melancholy reflection, that instead of praying over sermons, *many amuse themselves with them.* That which costs us many a prayer and many a tear is of no further worth to them than as giving an opportunity for exhibiting their critical abilities. I do not have to complain of any hard criticisms from you; you kindly approve of my poorest endeavors, and accept my feeblest words; I almost wish that some of you did not. Oh, that you would but kick against the truth! I might have some hopes for you, but alas for that indifference which makes you receive it all as a matter of course, and praise the style, and say you are thankful that the preacher is bold and honest with you, and thus the whole thing ends in your having complimented me without having sought my Master's favor. Oh, my hearer, we have something else to seek besides your good words. If you would hate *us,* we could not regret it if you would but love your own souls; but if you love us, and listen to our voice with respect, but nevertheless choose the downward path and go on to your own destruction, how can the preacher be content? Shall he go to his bed and remember that hundreds of you will dwell in everlasting burnings, and can never have a portion among the glorified spirits in heaven? Can he go to his bed and say, "It does not matter, they are pleased with me, and I am unto them as one that makes a sweet sound upon a goodly instrument"? Oh, I wish to God that instead of this you were brought like this poor blind man to go from hearing to praying, from your pews to your closets, from listening to me to communing with God, and seeking mercy at his hands.

You will say that you cannot fairly be classed in this category, for under the preaching of the Word *you have been led occasionally to pray.* Yes, and I do remember well when I myself was led to pray by hearing the Word. But what of it? The prayers of Sunday were forgotten in the sins of Monday, and the anxieties of the Sabbath were dissipated in the pleasures of the week. It is so with some of you. You pray when a sermon has been especially earnest. When the arrows of God wound you, you weep, and you promise change and a thousand fine things, and you even dream of flying to Christ, and taking hold upon the horns of the blood-sprinkled altar; but yet it is not done. You have made resolutions enough to pave the road to hell with them; you have piled up enough of your own professions to condemn you to an everlasting insolvency for bills dishonored and for debts unpaid. Oh, I wish to God you would be done with resolving and re-resolving, with these transient and temporary feelings! and oh, that these things would go right through your heart, leaving such wounds as none but Christ is able to heal! Oh, for the effectual work of God the Holy Spirit! What is the value of the cloud of the morning which flies before the gale, or the smoke of the chimney which is gone with the first puff? For eternity, you want something more lasting than the morning dew, something more substantial than chimney's smoke. O may the divine Spirit build you with his own right hand upon that good foundation: faith in the Lord Jesus Christ. The blind beggar, with but one sermon, and that exceedingly brief, never leaves off praying till Christ grants him his desire. May God give you also the desire to pray in earnest, lest you be sent to hell in earnest.

This poor man began to cry *for himself,* "*Son of David, have mercy on me!*" and we cannot bring men to hear for themselves. They will say, "I hope that sermon which was so appropriate to my friend will have a beneficial effect on him." You will think of those in the opposite gallery; your hearts will remember some sitting down below. Oh, mind yourselves! Another man's salvation is of course desirable, but what will it be to you that he would be in Abraham's bosom if you are with the rich man in the flames? Your own soul is that which you have to look to first. Self-preservation is a law of nature; be not disobedient to it! May grace put such force into it that from this day you will say, *"Son of David, have mercy on me!"* I confess to you that I could not read this passage without feeling the deepest and most humiliating feeling, to think that the mere report should have been so blessed to that man, and that year after year we should have given forth a much more full report of Christ Jesus, and yet have to say of many of you, *"Who has believed our report? And to whom has the arm of the Lord been revealed?"* I wish to God I could lay this more to my heart, and that you laid it more to your hearts, for, after all, it is more your concern than mine whether you are saved or not.

> The preacher is responsible for the faithfulness of his preaching, but hearers also are responsible for the earnestness of their hearing.

The preacher is responsible for the faithfulness of his preaching, but hearers also are responsible for the earnestness of their hearing, and God grant that your responsibility may not prove to be a millstone around your necks, to sink you to the lowest hell.

Passing onwards, we notice this man's intense desire as an absorbing passion.

There are many excuses which men make for themselves as to why they should not seek their soul's salvation just now. A very common one is, *"I am a very poor man. Religion is for the gentlefolks, for people that have time to spare, but it is of no use to a working man."* This person was a beggar. His position in life was far less honorable than yours, but, though a beggar, he desired that his eyes might be opened. And you, who are superior in your position to him, ought not to make the lowness of your condition an excuse for not seeking the salvation of your souls. Where did that lie first come from – the lie that the religion of Christ is not for the poor? Is it because so many of our sanctuaries are gorgeous in architecture? Is it because it is usual on Sunday, and very properly so, for people to put on their best clothes? And does the working man think that therefore he would not be welcome because he happens to be out of work, or has not a good suit of black to put on? Then by all means in the world let us break down this prejudice, and show to the working man that he is welcome here. I have often noticed you give a seat to a navigator or to a laborer in his work clothes when you have left very respectable people to stand in the aisles, and I do not blame you for it; well-dressed people may be less fatigued than those who have been toiling all week, so I admire the choice you make, because I hope it will go to prove that the working man is not a speckled bird among us. Why, it is all nonsense because we see a congregation well and respectably dressed to think that they must all necessarily belong to the upper classes. A certain preacher said to me the other day, "You preach to the rich, I preach to the poor." Now this was from lack of knowing better. We have, I am happy to say, some rich among us, whose princely gifts enable us to do much for the Lord's work; but still our great multitude is made up of the genuine working class. They are not an affectedly pious, whining lot, who will go about begging from everybody, and therefore dress shabbily. No, they are sober, saving people, and therefore, for the most part, they lift themselves out of the ditch of absolute poverty into manly independence. The religion of Christ is not for the poor man? Why, above all men, these are those that want it; and while the religion of Christ appeals to all ranks, if there be ever a preference given at all, it is the boast of the gospel of Christ that *"the poor have the gospel preached to them."* Now, do I have the ear of any man who has talked in that way and said, "It is all very well for gentlemen, and so on"? Now do not go and say that again, because you know it is not true. *You know it is not true.* We can give you thousands of instances where the religion of Jesus Christ blesses the cottage as much as ever it could bless the palace, and is found quite as useful to the laborer who has to toil from morning to night as to "My lady," who has next to nothing to do if she does not do something in the cause of Jesus Christ. Now get rid of that excuse.

Well, but this beggar might have said, "I must stick to my business." His business was begging, and though Jesus Christ might be passing by, he might very reasonably have said, "I really have no time to attend to this gentleman, whomever he may be. His preaching may be all very well and good, but I must beg right on, for when I get home there is little enough in my hat, and I really cannot afford the time to pay attention to this gentleman." That is what many people say: "Really, our business occupies all our time. We have to be always at it, early in the morning, almost before the sun is risen, and late at night till we are much too tired to read a book or to pray." Ah, but you see this man forgot his begging to find his eyesight, and you might well forget your trade to find your soul's sight. If it was worthwhile to neglect his begging to have his eyes opened, it would be worthwhile even if it were necessary to neglect your business if you might but find Christ; though, mark you, I do not believe that any man need neglect his lawful calling on account of religion.

Bartimaeus might have said, "I cannot pay attention to Jesus Christ now, for *it is the height of the season.*" You see, a beggar's season always is when plenty of people are about, and as Jesus had brought a crowd with him, he might very justly have said, "Why, if I do not beg now, it is of no use begging at any other time. I have a call of Providence to stick to my begging just now. I must attend to getting my eyes opened, if they can be opened, at some future time; but right now, I must make hay while the sun shines." This is your style of talking. "See! I am so very busy just now; providence has put a good thing in my way, and I must stick to it. I cannot be supposed to go out weeknights to hear sermons, and I cannot spare time for prayer. I want every moment that I can possibly get to make money, for now is my time. When I get old and can get a house in the country, I may then rest and attend to divine things." Ah! you simpleton! Here is a man who flings away the golden opportunity of gleaning money from the multitudes to seek his sight, and yet you are such a simpleton that you will not leave your gains to think of your eternal state.

He might have made yet other excuses if he would. For instance, he might have said, "Well, suppose I do get my eyes opened, then *I shall not be so well fitted for my trade as I now am,*" for a blind beggar gets twice as much as a man who can see; and it is rather a qualification to a beggar to have no eyes. Some of you feel, "If I had my soul saved, I could not trade as I now do. I know I should have to shut up that gin palace. I could not be the nurse of drunkenness, and yet call myself a Christian." "I could not stand at that bar," said a young woman to me who had been serving at one of the gin palaces. "The Lord had met with me, I did serve a few nights, but I could not stand it. I could not serve glasses of gin, and then go to the communion table – that would never do." There are some who are afraid to think about religion, because it will disqualify them for their business: and a blessed disqualification too – may the Lord disqualify thousands for the accursed work. But oh! if this man could well give up his poor trade of beggary to pray for his eyes, you may well give up your wicked trade if your souls may but enter heaven. If you should lose all the world, you have lost next to nothing if you have gained eternity.

I wonder that this man did not make the well-known excuse, "I do not know whether I am predestinated to have my eyes opened, because if I am to have my eyes opened, they will be opened, and if I am not to have my eyes opened, they will not be opened. So I shall sit still here, and hold my hat and beg. That is the main chance! I shall hold my hat and stick to my trade!" I do think that every man who uses this last excuse knows within himself that he is talking nonsense. I cannot believe in a rational man standing upright and saying, "If I am to be saved, I shall be saved, and therefore I shall not pray." I believe that man is a sneak; he is trying to make himself believe what he knows is not true. He knows very well that he does not say that kind of thing in business: "If I am to make twenty pounds, I shall make twenty pounds, and so I shall not take down the shutters tomorrow. If I am to have a harvest, I shall have a harvest, and so I shall not plow this year." He never does anything of the kind ordinarily, and yet he pretends he is such an idiot that he must throw away his soul because of the doctrine of predestination. Brethren, if a man means to hang himself, he can always find a piece of rope; and if a man means to damn himself, he can always find an excuse; and this excuse about predestination is one to which those run who are greater fools or wretches than ordinary. This man made no excuse of any sort whatever about his family, or his trade, or predestination, but he just cried out with vehemence, *"Son of David, have mercy on me!"*

We turn now to notice his vehemence, and observe that it was a most reasonable zeal.

It appears, according to the Greek, that this man had a good voice, or, at least, made the most of it. He did not sit and whisper, *"Son of David, have mercy on me"*; but he shouted, and, as the opposition increased, his shouts grew yet more loud: *"Son of David, have mercy on me!"* He was vehement and persevering in his prayer, but he was justified in his zeal. He was blind and *he knew the misery of blindness.* There are unutterable woes connected with it, and it needs much grace to make a man contented when his eye is closed to the light of day. This poor soul could not be content while there was a chance of a cure. But yours, sinner, is spiritual blindness – the blindness which does not let you see yourself or see your Savior, the blindness which shuts out all spiritual joys from your eyes, and will shut out the joys of heaven eternally from you, and condemn you to wander hopelessly in the blackness of darkness forever. However awfully earnest your prayers may be, they cannot be too earnest. *He was a beggar,* and *had doubtless learned the weakness of man.* He had often gone home with nothing when he had expected that his bag would be filled. And you too, you are a beggar. You have tried your own works and found them failing; you have begged at the door of ceremonies and you have found them to be an empty show; you have trusted first to one thing of man's invention and then to another, but after all your begging you still need heavenly charity to make you rich; you are naked and poor and miserable. Now, considering the weakness of man, and that Christ alone has power to save you, if your prayer should become as terribly earnest even as the shrieks of lost souls, it would be fully justified, for yours is an urgent, pressing case.

He knew, moreover, that Jesus Christ was near, and when Jesus Christ is near there is much cause for earnest prayer. If Jesus would not hear, if it were not a season of mercy, if grace were not being distributed plentifully, then you might be excused from praying; but oh! when it is a season of revival, when you are in the place where Jesus does bless souls, when you listen to the ministry which God has honored, then let your cry be more vehement than ever it has been. This poor man felt *it was now or never with him.* If he did not get his eyes opened that day, they might never be opened. Christ was passing by then and he might never pass that way again. Oh, sinner, it may be now or never with you. I know that God saves men at the eleventh hour, but I know also that there are many who are not saved at the eleventh hour, and that after such and such an hour has struck, many are given up to hardness of heart, permitted to be their own destroyers, without any restraints of conscience or of the Holy Spirit – and such may be your case. The ticking of the clock always cries to men who know how to interpret its meaning. "Now, or never! Now, or never! Today on earth, tomorrow in eternity!" If you wish to have Christ, the only time to seek him is today. *"Today if you hear His voice, do not harden your hearts."* Behold, **now** is *"the acceptable time,"* behold, **now** is *"the day of salvation"* (emphasis added). This the beggar felt, and therefore, up went the cry louder and yet more loud, *"Son of David, have mercy on me!"*

He guessed at least something of the value of sight. He had heard what others told him of the happiness of gazing upon the landscape, the field, the flood, and the sky. He longed to look into the face of friendship, and to know his own parent or his own child by sight. Well might he, if he guessed the value of his eyesight, cry most mightily. Sinner, you have at least a guess of the happiness of pardon. You have at least some idea of the sweetness of justification. You know, for you have often been told, that eternal life is well worth your seeking. Oh, man, may the Holy Spirit stir your heart till you can no longer restrain the cry, *"Jesus, Son of David, have mercy on me!"* I say, if you think of the dreadfulness of his present state, of the hope which the presence of Christ afforded him, and of the blessedness which he might expect from a restored eyesight, he had good reasons for being vehement. And, sinner, if you will think of the wrath of God abiding on you now, of the future with all its array of terror, and if you will remember the power of Christ to save, and the eternal blessedness of being safe in him, all these things, and especially the shortness of time and the present necessity of your case, should move you to cry yet more and more earnestly, *"Son of David, have mercy on me!"*

Let us pass on to a fourth point: this man experienced restraints in his prayer, and this is *a very common affliction.*

John Bunyan tells us that close to the wicket gate, Diabolus had a castle, and from this castle he used to shoot at all who sought an entrance. Moreover, he kept a big dog, which always barked and howled and sought to devour every person that knocked at the gate of mercy. I am sure that is true. Whenever a sinner gets to mercy's gate and begins knocking, that noise is heard in hell, and immediately the devil endeavors to drive the poor wretch away from the gate of hope. In the olden times, when the Algerian pirates took many Christian prisoners, they chained them to the oars of their galleys to row their masters. When Christian ships of war were seen in the distance, the captives knew that there was a hope of their being liberated; but their masters would come on deck and cry, "Pull for your lives," and the whip was laid on to make these poor captives fly by their efforts from their own rescue. This is what the devil does. He gets sinners to tug at the oar, and whenever Christ with his bloodred flag of liberty is seen within earshot, the sinner exerts himself to the utmost to get out of Christ's way. If that does not suffice, Satan will employ sometimes bad men and sometimes good men to stop the sinner from seeking a Savior at all. You know the ways in which *the world* will try to make a crying sinner hold his peace. The world will tell him that he is crying out about a matter that does not matter, for the book is not true; there is no God, no heaven, no hell, no hereafter. But if God has set you crying, sinner, I know you will not be stopped with that; you will cry yet the more exceedingly, *"Son of David, have mercy on me!"* Then the world will try pleasure; you will be invited to the theater; you will be attracted from one ballroom to another. But if the Lord puts the cry in your mouth, the intense anguish of your spirit will not be satisfied by the noise of musical instruments, nor by the shouts of those that make merry.

Perhaps the world will call you a fool to be vexed about such things; you are melancholy and have the blues. They will tell you that you will soon go where many others have gone – to Bedlam; but if once God has made you cry, you will not be stopped by a fool's laughter; the agonizing prayer will go up in secret: *"Have mercy on me!"* Perhaps the world will try its cares. You will be called into more business; you will get a prosperity which will not make your soul prosper; and so it will be hoped by Satan that you will forget Christ in accumulated wealth and growing cares. But ah! if this be such a cry as I hope it is, poor anxious sinner, you will not be stopped by that. Then the world will pretend to look down upon you with pity. Ah, poor creature, you are being misled, when you are being led to Christ and to heaven. They will say you have become the fool of some fanatic, when, in truth, you are now coming to your senses, and estimating eternal things at their proper value. Alas, but the worst is that even *the disciples* of Christ will act as these did in this narrative – they will charge you to "hold your peace."

Some professors have no sympathy for anxious souls. Much mischief is done by the light and frothy conversation of Christian professors, especially on the Sabbath day. How often sermons are blunted by a spirit of nitpicking. I have heard of a woman who prayed for her husband's conversion very earnestly, and one day, after the sermon, as she was walking home she was speaking to her friend and pulling the sermon to pieces. The doctrine did not quite suit her taste, and her husband looked at her with wonder. That sermon had broken his heart and yet here was a woman nitpicking at the very truth which God had blessed to give her the desire of her heart. I do not doubt that Christian people, by their unprofitable criticisms upon ministries which God has blessed, may mar the good work, and be the instruments in the hands of Satan of urging poor sinners to cease their cry. But oh, poor soul, let neither saint nor sinner make you stop. If you have begun to pray, though you have cried for months and no sweet answer of mercy has come, cry more loudly! Oh, be yet more earnest! Take the gates of heaven and shake them with your vehemence, as though you would pull them up post and bar and all. Stand at mercy's door, and take no denial. Knock, and knock, and knock again, as though you would shake the very spheres, but that you would obtain an answer to your cries. *"The kingdom of heaven suffers violence, and violent men take it by force."* Cold prayers never win God's ear. Draw your bow with your full strength, if you would send your arrow up so high as heaven. He whom God has taught to be resolved to be saved will be saved. He that will not take damnation as his fate, but who feels he must have Christ, is already under the divine operation of the eternal Spirit. Such a man bears the marks of divine election upon his very brow; such a man must and shall obtain everlasting salvation.

> He that will not take damnation as his fate, but who feels he must have Christ, is already under the divine operation of the eternal Spirit.

I come to the closing point. This man's urgency at last became so mighty that rebuffs became arguments with him.

He kept crying out all the more. He took the weapons out of their hands and used them on his own account. What do you suppose were the arguments that they used to induce him to stop praying? Would not one of them say, "Hold your tongue! You ragged, filthy beggar, hold your tongue!" "That is why I will not hold my tongue," says he. "I am such a poor disgusting object that I have need to cry. You gentlemen that are better off have no need to cry as I have; but the worse you prove me to be, the more need I have of the Master's help, and therefore I shall cry all the more." The devil says to you, "Do not pray, you are such a sinner." Tell the devil that is the reason why you will pray, for being so black, and foul, and filthy; these are all arguments as to why you above all other men should cry aloud, "Jesus, have mercy on me." Then they said, "Why, you have nothing to recommend you. Jesus Christ has not invited you; he has never looked on you with an eye of love, he has never called *you*." "Then it is the very reason," said he, "why I should call him. If I have no love token, then so much the worse for me, and so much the more reason why I should never be happy till I get one. If he has not invited me, then I will cry to him for an invitation." You see the more you can prove that the sinner's case is hopeless and bad, you have only proved that the sinner has the more reason for prayer. If I am the furthest from hope, why then he who wants to be heard, and is a very long way off, must call loudly; he that is further still, must call more loudly still; and he that is furthest off, must be the loudest of all. So if I am the furthest off from God and hope, I will only pray with the greater urgency till I do prevail.

"Alas, but," said another of them, "you make such a noise. Be still! you disturb the whole neighborhood." "Ah," says he, "I am thankful for that, for now *he* will hear me." I think this man, if he had heard the Savior tell the parable about the woman whose perpetual coming wearied the judge, must have said, "Make a noise, do I? So much the better; then I will make more, for I see I tease you. Perhaps I shall weary him, so I will even keep on till the judge is drawn to grant my request by the very noise I make." Some tell you that you should not be so earnest; why, you really disturb your friends; you have become so concerned about your soul that your friends are concerned about your sanity. Tell them you are glad of it and you mean to be more earnest, for if you have made hard-hearted man feel, you will soon make God, who bids us to give him no rest, at last give you the desire of your heart. Then they would say to him, "Now, do not disturb the Savior; he is so busy; he has so much to do. He is preaching now; he is talking to his disciples." "Ah, well," says he, "then if he does so many good things, the more reason why I should cry that he would do me a good turn also." It is of no use to ask a man to give anything who never gives anything, but the man who is always giving always will give; and so from Christ's many works he derives a reason why he should cry. "Is he blessing others? Then why not me?" So, dear hearer, when you hear of showers of blessings, ask that they may fall on you, and when you know that Christ is saving so many, make that a reason why he should save you, even you.

Then they said, "He is on a journey; he is going to Jerusalem; he cannot be stopped by every beggar. Hold your tongue! When do you think he will ever get there if he is to turn aside to every clamorous beggar who chooses to urge his claim?" "Traveling is he," said he, "then I will stop him now, for if I once let him go by I shall never catch him again. Going to Jerusalem to die! Ah, then my hope will be all over. I have him now; I will not give him a chance of going by." Louder goes up the cry, *"Son of David, have mercy on me!"* If the devil tells you "It is too late!" then say, "I will go directly; I will not stop. If so many years have passed over my head without my finding a Savior, then every one of these shall be a spur to make me fly like the wind more swiftly."

It is very likely that they also said to him, "How dare you, a beggar, interrupt such a person as Jesus Christ? Why, he is going in triumph through Jerusalem. He is to ride with solemn pomp all through the streets. What can you be at, thinking that you are to have an audience with such a great one as he is?" "Great one! is he?" the man seemed to say. "Great one! I want a great one! A little one will not serve my turn. It must be a great one that can open my eyes, and the greater he is the more reason why I should cry to him." So whenever you are alarmed at the glory and greatness of the Lord Jesus Christ, do not be put back because of that, but rather say, "Is he mighty? Then he is mighty to save. Is he a Savior and a great one? Then he is just such a Savior as I want. I will never rest; I will never pause till he says unto my soul, 'I am your salvation.'"

Now I did solemnly ask of God that he would today excite in some sinner a desire to pray, and that if there were one here who had been praying and who was tempted to cease, the Word might be blessed by God the Holy Spirit to make him more incessant in his prayer. O may he grant my petition.

Remember that the only way in which this praying and this waiting will come to an end is by looking alone to Jesus Christ. If you turn that eye of yours away from yourself and your feelings, and turn your prayers to Jesus Christ's finished work, and trust him, you will find peace directly. There is peace to the soul that looks only to Jesus. While I have been exhorting you to pray, and I meant to do it earnestly, more earnestly than I have been able to do it, I did not wish you to put praying in the place of believing. If you cannot as yet understand Christ so as to rest on him, if you cannot as yet cast yourself on him, then pray for more enlightenment, pray to be led to faith, and pray that faith may be given to you. But oh, may God give you the power and the will now, even now, to exert a living faith upon the crucified Savior, for there is "life in a look at the Crucified One." Praying will ultimately bring you to that point, but I pray God to bring you to it now through his mighty Spirit, and so like Bartimaeus, may we receive our sight and follow Jesus along the way, and to Jesus be the glory forever and ever. Amen.

Chapter 3

Jesus Stops

And Jesus stopped. (Mark 10:49)

A friend inquired of me yesterday, "Will you preach on Sunday morning to saints or to sinners?" I could not at the moment answer him, but I afterwards thought within myself, If I preach concerning Jesus Christ, our Lord and Savior, I shall kill two birds with one stone, and give both saints and sinners a profitable theme for thought. There is but one message of the gospel, and it has a voice to all. Saints know no sweeter music than the name of Jesus, and sinners know no richer comfort than his person and his work. We preach to all when we preach him who is all in all. Christ comes as life to the dead, and he is equally life to the living. I trust there will at this time be a word in season, both to those who fear God and to those who fear him not, while I speak of the Savior from these three words: *And Jesus stopped.*

Our divine Lord has changed his position, but he is himself the same as ever, and therefore every truth which we learn concerning him in the past becomes all the more valuable since it is still true of him today. Our Lord's name is *Jesus Christ . . . the same yesterday and today and forever.* What his character was on earth, such it is still; his pursuits on earth are his pursuits still; his main object when he was here is his chief aim even in glory. We do not have to say, "This is what Jesus was," and then to mourn that he has changed; for he is without variableness. His transit from the tree to the throne has not affected his nature so as to make him other than he was when here below. If we delight in a trait of his character as drawn in the Gospels, we may be sure that he possesses the same excellence now that he is at the right hand of the Father.

His dealing with blind Bartimaeus nineteen centuries ago is a fair type of his conduct towards every poor blind sinner who at this hour comes to him crying, *"Son of David, have mercy on me!"* I hope we shall see the miracle of Jericho repeated in this house this very day. I am persuaded that it will be so; for even now, constrained by the prayers already offered, Jesus waits to be gracious; and today it shall be said that at the entreaties of his people Jesus paused to work wonders of love – *And Jesus stopped.*

First, let us answer this question – What is the meaning of this pause in the Savior's progress: *And Jesus stopped.* This was not his frequent posture; for he was ever on the move: *He went about doing good.* He might have done much among men if he had taken up his station and remained in one place, so that the crowds could have resorted to him to listen to his voice, or to be healed by his power. But Jesus was not an immovable statue of benevolence; he was active and energetic, an itinerant preacher who never wearied in his circuit. One does not often see Jesus stopping. His was the love which does not wait to be sought after by men, for it has come to seek as well as to save that which was lost. The zeal of the Lord's house consumed him, so that for him there was no loitering or stopping. Yet in the case before us the Great Worker ceased from his activity: *And Jesus stopped.*

In the Gospel we read that our Lord was going up to Jerusalem with his face steadfastly set to accomplish his great work. His own words were, *"Behold, we are going up to Jerusalem, and the Son of Man will be delivered to the chief priests and the scribes; and they will condemn Him to death and will hand Him over to the Gentiles. They will mock Him and spit on Him, and scourge Him and kill Him, and three days later He will rise again"* (Mark 10:33-34.) He had a baptism to be baptized with, and he was distressed until it was accomplished; therefore, with brave resolve he forced his way to the city. Every pause to him would have been untimely unless there had been some weighty reason to stall him. His great work pressed upon his soul, and he longed to be fully engaged in it, as one who has a cup to drink and thirsts to set it to his lips.

Yet, though his thoughts were thus urgently preoccupied, and his whole heart engrossed, we find him pausing in his steady progress to the desired end; *and Jesus stopped*. There was, doubtless, something somewhat special about this recorded pause. What was it which fastened him to the spot? It was not hesitancy – his resolve was too firm; it was not fear – the thought of drawing back never passed the Redeemer's mind. Onward, onward, was his fixed resolve. He stood still from no unworthy motive; all his movements and his pauses have a nobility about them and a fullness of meaning which no personal motive can account for.

Our Lord was beginning at the moment that triumphal procession which continued till he reached the temple amid the hosannas of the multitude. It is true he was advancing to the cross; but before he reached his death he was to be proclaimed as the King, meek and lowly, who came riding upon a colt, the foal of a donkey. His triumphal march has begun, and Jesus is in the midst of admiring listeners. Yet Jesus stands still; the whole procession halts; the twelve disciples and the company of the faithful are stopped, and the crowd waits in the roadway of Jericho. For what great reason did it happen that Jesus stood still? I could have wished that a master sculptor had been there and could then have caught a glimpse of the standing Jesus. I think I see him suddenly stopped; he moves not an inch, but waits in listening attitude. His eye is fixed in the direction from where had come a certain pleading cry. His ears are evidently open to hear the movement which follows his command to call the petitioner.

The Savior's thoughts are pausing too; he stands still mentally as well as physically, engrossed by one object to which he will pay attention before he takes another step. Ceasing from his discourse, however much his hearers regret his silence, he gives ear, and eye, and tongue to the petitioner whose voice reached him above the tramping and hubbub of the crowd. *That cry came from a blind beggar – that was the man.* Yes, the blind beggar of Jericho had stopped the prophet of Nazareth: say his name – blind Bartimaeus, the son of Timaeus, has stopped the

Savior and holds him spellbound. Jesus waits in perfect readiness to attend to the pleading one and grant him his desire. The cry of *"Son of David, have mercy on me!"* has caught his ear, and the music of the word *mercy* holds him. As the Song of Solomon has put it, *The king is held in the galleries.* Attentive and prepared to help with all his mighty power, Jesus waits. He waits at a blind beggar's prayer, resolved to do his bidding. I have seen servants wait upon their masters, but here is the Lord of all waiting upon one lower than a servant, waiting upon a blind man whose trade was begging.

And Jesus stopped. He was all there: ready, willing, and able, too, to do for the poor man whatsoever he needed. He asked him, *"What do you want Me to do for you?"* as if he stood at his beck and call and could not take a step onward until he had answered the prayer.

And Jesus stopped. I have heard of Joshua who said, *"O sun, stand still at Gibeon, and O moon in the valley of Aijalon"*; but I rank the blind beggar above Joshua, for he causes the Sun of Righteousness to stand still. Yes, he who created both sun and moon stood still, and the Lord hearkened to the voice of a man. Jericho had produced in ages long ago a prodigy of faith among her harlots, and now she shows us a wonder of grace among her beggars. How marvelous was the power which dwelt in that poor man's cry! Is such power to be found among men at this hour? Ah, there is the point. The Savior is the same today as ever, and I believe, my brethren, that you and I have power at this time to make him stop and stand still if we act as Bartimaeus did.

Many a poor sinner here today, if God shall help him to cry after the style of the blind man, can command the Savior's full attention, can command his power, and can get from him the grace which he is so willing and able to bestow. As for you who know and love him, be well assured that no blind beggar can have such power with him as you have who are his friends. I am sure that the voices of those who have laid their heads in his bosom must have great power over him, and if our brethren will but use their influence with the Well-beloved they may ask what they will, and it shall be done unto them. Pleading saints can cause him to stand still even now. I have feared and trembled for my country of late, lest the Lord Jesus should depart from it and take away the candlestick out of its place. More than two hundred years ago George Herbert said, when he looked upon the declining state of godliness in England,

> Religion stands a-tiptoe in our land,
> Ready to pass to the American strand.

He saw the Puritans flying away to the New England colonies, and he trembled for the ark of God in his own land; but, thank God, the prayers of Herbert and the prayers of other saints have constrained the Lord Jesus to abide with us, though *He acted as though He were going farther.* Brethren, the Lord had thought, as it were, to cross the Atlantic, and fix his dwelling among a people who would be gathered in a newly discovered land. Thank God, he has built a church in America; but he has not left us without witness. Because of the tears of his saints, *Jesus stopped.* Still, we hold him, and we will not let him go; he abides among our churches, still opening blind eyes, saving souls, and making men whole. O you that love him, take care that by your entreaties you still detain him.

At times our Lord, as judge among the nations, arises to visit the sins of a people upon them. Patience makes room for justice, and Providence determines that guilty nations shall be scourged; at such times they are blessed indeed who can cause the King to stand still. This wicked country of ours has often escaped through the prayers of the saints. No man can read our history without perceiving that among guilty nations we hold a sorrowful place; for we have had more light than any other people, and have sinned against it very often. This erring nation would have been scourged to destruction if it had not been that the intercessions of God's people have caused the judge of all the earth to stand still. Jesus now rules all nations as Lord of Providence, and metes out justice and judgment among them. But a plea for mercy brings a decree of patience, and sinful nations are permitted still to stand within the bounds of grace.

I doubt not that when the end of a reprobate has almost come, and when a sinner's breath has almost left his body, and the judgment has been about to be executed upon his guilty soul, the prayers of earnest men and women have made the merciful One linger yet a little longer, and give a further space in which repentance might spring up in the long-hardened heart, and the faith-glance might yet be given by the long-blinded eye. What pauses grace has made when faith has interceded!

Whatever our Lord Jesus is doing he is never so occupied as to disregard earnest prayer. He would, if needful, put everything aside to listen to compelling and earnest pleading. To this day Jesus stands still to hear the cry of the destitute. If at this moment we could withdraw the curtains of heaven, we would see our Savior waiting to be gracious, ready to hear our prayers, hearkening to every sigh, putting every tear into his bottle, and answering every petition which comes up before him from a sincere heart. Though he rules empires, he stands still to hear the wailing of distress; though he inhabits the praises of Israel, he is moved by the sorrows of sinners; though he hastens the day of his coming, and is ready to begin his triumphal advent to the New Jerusalem, yet will he pause when the poor and needy present their case before him.

Thus have I tried to picture the Lord Jesus as standing still. How I wish that some awakened one would now behold the Savior and exclaim, with Mr. Wesley,

> Stopp'd by a sinner's prayer,
>   Thou canst no farther move,
> Thou canst no more forbear
>   To manifest thy love.
> Thou waitest now to show thy grace,
>   And callest me to seek thy face.

We will now enter upon a practical inquiry: Who and what was this which suddenly caught the Savior? What made him stop? Herod could not have done it, nor Pilate, nor the chief priests, nor the scribes, nor the foresight of the bloody sweat, nor a vision of the cross. These would but have hastened his steps to enter upon the conflict and achieve redemption. What made him stop?

First, as I have already said, it was *a blind beggar*. I am afraid there are very few here today who are literally beggars; for nowadays we wear good clothes, and are so very respectable that spiritlessly poor people do not like to come and sit with us. The greater is the pity. Yet

I know that many poor persons are here now, and I thank God that it is so. Those who are in the depths of poverty will, I hope, believe that they are welcome to the house of the Lord, who is no respecter of persons. We are very glad to see the poor among us, the more the merrier. Bartimaeus was a man of the very lowest order; he did not earn his own bread, he could not. He sat publicly by the wayside and held out his hand for charity. Men give small honor to a blind beggar, and are apt to pass him by without regard; but he to whom we owe all hope of heaven stood still at the cry of such as he.

After this no one among you will dare to say, "I cannot be saved because I am so obscure, so poor, so homeless, so helpless." Tell me what you are at your very worst, and still I have good tidings concerning my Lord's condescending favor to the likes of you. Did you lodge in the casual ward last night? Yet are you welcome to Christ. Have you come from the workhouse? Yet are you invited to the palace of grace. Do you labor very hard for very little, and can you barely pay your way? The Lord Jesus Christ wants no fee or reward from you; come empty-handed to his treasury. Jesus does not look at garments. What does Christ care about our coats? Tailors think of such matters, but Jesus does not. Christ sees the man himself and not his clothing; he looks not at the man's possessions, but at his heart. In mercy he beholds not the excellence of the man, but his needs, his sorrows, and his poverty.

The Lord Jesus Christ wants no fee or reward from you; come empty-handed to his treasury.

No man here shall ever be able to say, "It was of no use for me to think about religion, for my circumstances were too low." "I was depressed," says one. "I should have thought about better things, but really the grind of poverty was so dreadful that I could not rise from the dust." This is not true, for you are not poorer than the blind beggar of Jericho, and the sharp tooth of poverty has not bitten you more severely than many of the Lord's suffering saints. Misery had eaten into the heart of this poor blind man, and yet his cry made the Savior stop. Now then, you that are the lowest, poorest, most afflicted, most despised in this house, I pray that you may be helped to appeal to Jesus for mercy, and he will stop to listen to you, even to you.

But what was the art by which Bartimaeus stopped the Lord? That which stopped the Savior was *a blind beggar's cry*. The man did not sing a touching hymn to a melting tune, he only cried. Sometimes persons have such melodious voices that if they sing in the street you linger to hear them, and are in no hurry to go on with your errand. But this man did not sing; he had not even learned to chant his prayers as certain ones do in these odd times. I wonder whether the Lord ever listens to prayers when men turn them into singsong and deliver them in an unnatural voice – *intoning* they call it. Why do men think it an improvement to say their prayers the wrong way upwards? This man *cried*. It was a cry, a ringing cry, which increased in strength each time it was uttered. Thus it rose up into the ear: *"Son of David, have mercy on me!" "Son of David, have mercy on me!"* The voice came from a heart burdened with misery, breaking with desire, weary of long years of darkness, pining for the light, and hopeful of obtaining it. *"Son of David, have mercy on me!"* again the cry rose above all the hubbub of the throng.

The prayer was *a cry for mercy: "Son of David, have mercy."* If you ask our Lord for anything on the grounds of merit, you will find him deaf as a stone. If you think yourself a very good person, deserving favor at his hands, he will pass on and never regard you, for he has not come to call the righteous, but sinners to repentance. Change that plea for the better, for when your prayer is for mercy you will touch the Savior's heart directly, and mercy shall be yours. The proud man prays, and he thinks his eloquent prayer must prevail, but the winds carry away his supplications; the humble man does no more than strike his breast and say, *"God, be merciful to me, a sinner!"* and that cry for mercy wins the day.

When the messenger of mercy was traveling through the world he asked himself what inn he should stop at and spend the night. Lions and Eagles were not on his mind, and he passed by houses wearing such warlike names; so too he passed by places known by the sign of "The Waving Plume" and "The Conquering Hero," for he knew that there was no room for him in these inns. He hastened by many inns and did not delay till at last he came to a little inn which bore the sign of "The Broken Heart." "Here," said mercy's messenger, "I would willingly wait, for I know by experience that I shall be welcome here." *A broken and a contrite heart, O God, You will not despise.* Now, beloved friends, if you plead for mercy because you are deeply conscious that nothing but the grace of God can save you, even though you cannot put pretty words together or offer a long prayer, you shall prevail with God. You need not be an orator in order to be mighty in pleading with the Lord. Only appeal on the grounds of free grace and dying love, and Jesus will stop and listen to you.

There was another point about this cry which must not be forgotten: *the name of Jesus was used as a plea.* Is there anything in heaven, or out of heaven, more powerful than the name of Jesus? *"Whatever you ask of the Father in My name He may give to you." "Whatever you ask in My name, that will I do."* Father and Son stand pledged to recognize and accept every draw upon the resources of heaven which is endorsed with the name of Jesus, a name that makes angels rejoice and devils tremble; there is none like it anywhere. The blind beggar of Jericho had learned to use the name of Jesus, and he called him *"Son of David"* – Prince, Messiah, the sent One of God, the Savior of the world.

Herein is wisdom. O dear hearer, if you know the name of Jesus, plead it; if you know what he is, what he came to do, what he has done, what he is doing; if you know anything about his character, his nature, his power, or his promise, plead it before him in prayer. In humble faith say to him, "Son of David, if you be indeed all this, be all this to me, I beg you. If you are a Savior, save *me.* If you blot out sin, blot out mine. If you do open the eyes of understanding, open mine, for your great mercy's sake." When we can thus reason together with the Lord, we shall have good success in his presence, and again it shall be said, *Jesus stopped.*

I suppose the main thing which brought our gracious Master to a stop was the fact that he had now *an opportunity for doing good.* Jesus has come to seek his lost sheep, and when his eyes light upon one all torn and lame he stops to deal tenderly with it. Our Lord was an itinerant Savior, and wherever he found that he was wanted, there he stayed. The object of his mission is still the same:

> He comes, from thickest films of vice,
>   To clear the mental ray;
> And on the eyeballs of the blind
>   To pour celestial day.
>
> He comes, the broken heart to bind,
>   The bleeding soul to cure;
> And, with the treasures of his grace,
>   To enrich the humble poor.

Certain people in his day boasted that they could see. Our Lord did not wait to argue with them; they did not want him, and he therefore passed them by. But here is a blind man, and was it not said of the Messiah that he could open the eyes of the blind? Here is the opportunity for him, and before that opportunity he stands still until his illuminating work shall be done. You good people who imagine that you will go to heaven by your own works, my Lord does not wait on you; but you poor sinners who have no merits, you guilty ones who need his mercy, Jesus stops for you. You who have so much strength, that you can believe when you like, can repent when you like, can be saved when you like, can be quite independent of the Holy Spirit and the sovereign grace of God, yet Jesus does not look at you. But oh, you that are blind and cannot see, you that wish you could see, you who groan because you have no strength, you are the men for my Master. Believe me, the Lord of mercy looks not at merit, but at misery. The necessity of the case is its claim upon his tender heart. O sons of men, the infinite Savior cares not for your fullness; his eye of pity rests upon your emptiness. He turns indignantly from delusional claims of proud, self-righteous men, but he hastens to relieve those who confess their faults and seek his face. This is the work and office of Jesus, and he loves to exercise his high calling. Come to him, and put your case into his hand. Be this your prayer:

Since still thou goest about to do
    Thy needy creatures good;
On me, that I thy praise may show,
    Be all thy wonders show'd.

If thou, my God, art passing by,
    Oh, let me find thee near!
Jesus, in mercy hear my cry,
    Thou, Son of David, hear!

Behold me waiting, in the way,
    For thee, the heavenly light;
Command me to be brought, and say,
    "Sinner, receive thy sight."

Thus I have tried to show what was the power which riveted the Savior to the spot so that the gospel said, *Jesus stopped.*

Under our third topic we shall now inquire – What was there that was special about this blind man and his prayer? An answer lies on the surface – there was this that was special about it: first, that *the man was full of need.* He had two loads to carry. He was poor – that is bad enough, but he was also blind – that is worse. Here was a man with a double need, without bread and without light; and therefore his cries had a double loudness in the ears of the Sinner's Friend.

I cannot so look around these galleries and over this area as to spy out those in direst need, or I would look their way and say, "Come, you sinners, poor and wretched"; but I can make a few inquiries, and may the Lord find out his own by them. Is there anyone here who has a double need, who is doubly guilty, doubly helpless – a man who feels that if Jesus does not save him, he will be doubly damned? Do I speak to one whose need is doubly pressing, so that his heart breaks for immediate relief? Ah, you doubly lost one, Jesus will stop for you. You who are blind and poverty-stricken too, shall have a speedy audience. You that have nothing, and can see no hope of ever having anything, you are the favored ones whose pleading voices Jesus never disregards.

Cry mightily to him at once. He waits at this moment. "Why," says one, "you are preaching up our poverty, our poverty, and our bankruptcy." Exactly so.

> 'Tis perfect poverty alone
>   That sets the soul at large;
> While we can call one mite our own
>   We get no full discharge.
>
> But let our debts be what they may,
>   However great or small,
> As soon as we have nought to pay,
>   Our Lord forgives us all.

But there was another specialty about this man besides his double need, and that was *his strong desire.* When he sought for sight he meant it, and there was no question about his sincerity and eagerness. His was no prayer which froze on the lips. His desire was, moreover, a very fitting and appropriate one. He sighed not for a luxury, but for a necessity. Our Lord said in the thirty-sixth verse of Mark chapter 10 to James and John, *"What do you want Me to do for you?"* and now, when he speaks to Bartimaeus, he uses the same words – *"What do you want Me to do for you?"* James and John asked what was not fitting, or needful, or proper; but this poor man had a desire which was, of all others, the most natural and suitable. What should a blind man seek but sight? Have you, dear hearer, a longing for salvation? What else should a sinner long for? Do you desire forgiveness of sin? It is of all things most fitting that a guilty one should desire pardon. Do you wish for an opened spiritual eye? Do you pray to be made whole? Do you long to become holy? Oh, then, if your desire be real and fervent, its object is so suitable and so commendable that you may be sure of its being granted; therefore, be of good cheer, and at this moment hope in the Lord.

Another thing that was special about the case was *the man's earnest pleading,* for his desire turned itself into prayer, and that prayer took up arguments and urged them earnestly. His prayer was so full of life that it could not be repressed. Many tried to silence his cry, but it could not be hushed. Important persons said to the man, "Be quiet." Apostles charged him to hold his tongue, but he heeded no one. I am sure that if an apostle were to say to some of you, "Do not pray," you would feel quite warranted in ceasing from praying; at least, it would serve as a good-enough excuse for you. You would say, "I never mean to seek mercy anymore, for Peter told me not to do so."

Oh, but if in your heart there is a work of grace, fifty Peters could not stop your praying. Irrepressible prayer brings assured answers. If there is a prayer in your soul that James and John could not silence, if there is a cry in your soul that Andrew and Bartholomew and Nathanael and the whole eleven of them could not suffocate, the Lord Jesus will speedily hear you. Pray, my brethren, pray without ceasing, though all the devils in hell should charge you not to pray. Though all the saints in heaven should vote your pleading useless, yet still plead on, and your appeal shall succeed with the Redeemer. He stops for you, and even now it may be said of him, *Jesus stopped*.

That, after all, which fastest bound the Savior was *the man's faith*, for he said to him, *"Your faith has made you well."* What kind of faith was it? It was the best faith as to origin, for it was the faith of a blind man, and therefore was not adulterated by the confidence which comes by sight. Faith comes not by seeing, or else it never could have come to this poor beggar; it comes by hearing, and he could hear. We have among us a certain sort of people who seem to imagine that faith comes by sight. Acting upon this, they work upon the eye in many ways. If you step inside the walls of their churches you see an enormous cross; the altar is sumptuously adorned; mystical letters and characters are here and there in abundance. Open your eyes and get a blessing, if there be one. See, here comes a man who on his back and all around him carries means of grace for the eye. He wears an embroidered cross, and all over he is rigged out and ragged out, so as to instruct and save all who are willing to study symbolic clothes. He that has eyes to see let him see. Watch what this successor of the apostles is doing; observe his genuflections, his facings about, his noddings of the head – all these minister grace to the beholders.

> **Faith comes not by seeing, or else it never could have come to this poor beggar; it comes by hearing.**

Faith of the High Anglican kind would seem to come by sight, but the faith of God's elect – the faith which saves the soul – *comes from hearing, and hearing by the word of Christ.* Bartimaeus had seen nothing, but he had believed the report concerning the Messiah, and had received the benediction: *"Blessed are they who did not see, and yet believed."* If Jesus Christ raised the dead, this man did not see the miracle; if Jesus healed the leper, this man did not see the wonder; and if the lame man leaped like a deer, this man had neither seen his crutches nor his leaping: his faith was solely born of hearing, and this is faith's best pedigree. Dear friends, be attentive hearers of the gospel. Thank God that you are privileged to be hearers. You need not sigh for ceremonials or architecture or processions. If you are a hearer of the gospel you have sufficient means of grace. By the Eargate, King Jesus rides into the town of Mansoul. He says, *"Incline your ear and come to Me. Listen, that you may live."* What! Though no dream, or vision, or rapturous experience be as a sign for your eye to see, believe in Jesus and you shall find in him more than all signs and wonders.

Thus have we thought over the peculiar forces which made the Savior stop; may we know how to use them. Does anyone ask, What does this have to do with us? This is my last point: "What is there special for you, my hearer?" I think there may be much for you, for it contains much for me. I was a blind beggar once, as blind as the heathens' gods, of which we read, *They have eyes, but they cannot see;* and I was a beggar too, so penniless as not to possess a pennyworth of merits to bless myself with. I thought I had some good works once, quite a little cupboard full, but they bred worms and stunk, and I had to sweep them all out and sweeten the place which they had defiled. I found myself worse than having nothing, for, like the Egyptians when the plague of frogs was removed, I had heaps of rubbish to get rid of. My former good works became, in my judgment, like forged banknotes or counterfeit money: I was afraid of being charged with the attempt to utter them. Alas, my detestable good works, my proud good works, my deceitful good works pressed heavily on my conscience.

By putting these into the place of Christ I had made them worse than my sins. I was in a worse state than a man who owns nothing, for I was head over heels in debt, and I knew it. Then it was that I heard of one who would deliver me, and I cried to him, and he delivered me speedily. Oh, how I wish that many others would feel that they too need the divine Savior. O that men knew that they are poor, and blind, and that Jesus can give them eyes, and can supply all their wants.

It is a very curious thing – a very curious thing to me – that so much uncertainty hangs over this narrative. I am not so sure as to speak positively, but I believe that this story which Mark tells us is not the whole of what happened, for Matthew is certain that there were two blind men. Hear what Matthew says about it. Surely it is the same incident, or one strangely similar. Matthew 20:29-33: *As they were leaving Jericho, a large crowd followed Him. And two blind men sitting by the road, hearing that Jesus was passing by, cried out, "Lord, have mercy on us, Son of David!" The crowd sternly told them to be quiet, but they cried out all the more, "Lord, Son of David, have mercy on us!" And Jesus stopped and called them, and said, "What do you want Me to do for you?" They said to Him, "Lord, we want our eyes to be opened."* There were two blind beggars, though Mark only sees it needful to mention the principal one. If there were two, one of them is not known by name at all. We know the name of Bartimaeus, and we know the name of his father, but we do not know the name of his companion. Mark might have left out the father's name, which is implied in the name of Bartimaeus, and he might have mentioned the other beggar, but he was not moved so to do, perhaps for the very reason that we should learn more from his silence than from the information.

I reverence the silence of the Bible as much as its speech. I have been wondering if there be a man or woman here who will be saved today of whom we shall never hear, whose name will never be on our books, and whose story will never cheer our heart. It appears from what Matthew says that this No. 2, whoever he was, this anonymous body, prayed in the same words as Bartimaeus.

Bartimaeus was a man of force and energy, and he made his prayer the same in its words: *"Son of David, have mercy on me!"* The other man followed suit, and adopted the methods of Bartimaeus. He was like the poor orator who had to speak after Burke, and very wisely said no more than "I say ditto to Mr. Burke." Mark does not take much notice of him, because he was the echo of Bartimaeus, and probably a poor, feebleminded lazybones, whose only chance seemed to be in following the lead of a stronger mind. Here, then, is the mercy of it, that though we do not know the man's name, he had his eyes opened quite as surely as Bartimaeus did, and though he could not make a prayer of his own, and only followed Bartimaeus, he had sight of his own, and a word of comfort for himself from Jesus.

Oh, poor dear hearts, you right away in the background there, you that never will have the courage to join the church because you are so timid, be of good courage, for Jesus observes even you. Oh, you poor trembling ones, who have not sense enough to put a dozen words together – at least you think so, for there is no telling what may be hidden away in you somewhere – remember that it is the inward desire that Jesus hears, and not the pleasing sentences of ready speakers. If you can only pray as somebody else prayed, I would have you borrow your prayers from the Bible, for scriptural prayers are sure to be right. Take the prayer of the publican if you cannot make one of your own, and say, *"God, be merciful to me, the sinner!"*

As soon as I saw that there were two beggars whose eyes were opened, I thought, "After preaching I will look to meet with a convert whose name and family I shall know, and with his tale of grace I will solace myself; but oh, that my Lord would bless some whom I shall never know, some anonymous ones, some nobodies, some weak and shrinking souls. Are there any such as this here? Will not many such as this *read* the sermon? O that at their cry Jesus may stand still to bless them.

I must mention a more curious thing still. I am not certain, I am not clear, I am talking about things which must remain undecided – but it is very possible that there were *three* blind beggars healed. It may be that first of all one man, Bartimaeus, appealed to the Lord Jesus and had his eyes opened when Jesus was nearly out of Jericho; and then two others had their eyes opened when Jesus and the crowds were actually going out of the town. Many writers think that Matthew and Mark record two different incidents, and it is very likely to be so. Probably the two blind men, having heard of the success of Bartimaeus, were encouraged to try for themselves, and carefully imitated his model, crying in the same language for the same aid. Thus there was a repetition of the incident on a doubled scale. I like that notion. I wonder whether

No. 3 is here, whose name we do not know, and probably never shall know, but yet he is known to Jesus and his cry is heard. He has come here with poor No. 2, who is equally weak and trembling with himself: God bless them both.

Those of us on whom the Savior has worked a good work would speak well of him for the encouragement of the fearing ones. I bear my witness to the eye-opening power of the gospel. *"One thing I do know, that though I was blind, now I see,"* and no one opened my eyes but Jesus. I went to him just as I was; I trusted him and he saved me. May there not be two more blind men or women sitting somewhere around here who will follow our example? Just do as we have done, pray and trust, cry and believe. Say, "Lord, Son of David, have mercy on me!" Remember, he who has saved one can save two; he who has saved two can save three. Alas, it stops not at three. If there were three thousand here, who all cried for mercy, they would all have it, and as would many millions more as could be found to follow in the same track.

I see today before my mind's eye Jesus standing before Jericho like a second Joshua. As you all know, the names *Jesus* and *Joshua* are the same. Joshua crossed the Jordan, and he stood with his sword drawn to capture Jericho, and commence his march through Canaan, conquering and to conquer. See, here is Jesus, and he must make captives in Jericho before he advances further into the land. The city of palm trees must yield him followers before the palms of victory are cast at his feet. He enters Jericho, not to lay its walls flat to the ground, nor to slay its inhabitants, but to open eyes that have long been closed, and to bless poor creatures who have languished in poverty. This is the first fruit of his warfare, the commencement of a career which shall end at Jerusalem, where he shall strike the Prince of Darkness, and win the victory for all mankind.

Even now I may say of Jesus Christ that which was said of the son of Nun – *So the Lord was with Joshua, and his fame was in all the land.* I wish the Lord Jesus Christ would make this place as the gate of Jericho, and begin on this spot a great revival of religion throughout the whole land, by opening the eyes of some that are blind. Let the prayer go up from many a heart, "Lord, open my eyes," and he will do it; and let that request be followed by another: "Lord, save millions," and he will hear us. Let us pray boldly and believingly in the name of Jesus. Hear us, O Lord. Amen.

Chapter 4

A Gospel Sermon to Outsiders

"Take courage, stand up! He is calling for you." (Mark 10:49)

No doubt a large number of believers are here, many of them well-established in the faith, who would like to hear a doctrine argued, a type interpreted, or an apocalyptic symbol unfolded, but really I cannot do that now. I feel something like Luther when preaching to a mixed assembly. He said, as nearly as I can remember, words to this effect: "I perceive in the church Dr. Justus Jonas, and Melancthon, and other learned doctors. Now, if I preach to their edification, what is to become of the rest? Therefore, by their leave, I shall forget that Dr. Jonas is here at all, and preach to the multitude." So must I do at this good hour, asking those of you who are advanced in the divine life to unite your prayers with mine, which will continually ascend, that the word of the gospel may be blessed to the unconverted.

Dear friends, there are so many of you that have been for years listening to the proclamation of the gospel, those on the border, almost in Emmanuel's land but not quite – that I feel most earnest that this night should be the time of your decision for the Savior – that you should not remain any longer hearers only, but should become believers immediately, and afterwards doers of the Word. There are gentlemen in England who can afford to drive a coach and tour from town to town and carry nobody, performing their journeys for their own amusement; but I am not able or willing to do anything of that kind. Unless I can have my coach loaded with passengers to heaven, I would sooner it was never started, and had rather my team stopped in the stable. We must carry some souls to heaven, for our call is from above, and our time is too precious to throw away on mere pretense of doing good. We cannot play at preaching: we preach for eternity. We cannot feel satisfied merely to deliver sermons to senseless throngs, or to the most attentive crowds. Whatever smiles may greet us as we start, and whatever salutations may welcome us at our close, we are not content unless Jesus works salvation by us. Our desire is that grace should be magnified, and that sinners should be saved.

They used to jeer at the tabernacle in Moorfields, and the one in Tottenham Court Road, and call them Mr. Whitfield's soul traps – a very excellent name for a place of worship; such may this tabernacle ever be! It ought to be a soul trap, and we shall be disappointed, indeed, if there are not some souls taken in the trap today. If God does not bless the Word and make it so potent that some of you shall really close in with the gospel proclamation and enter into eternal life, I shall be heavy of heart.

Before I attempt to deal with my text, let me describe to you the plan of salvation. You know it, the most of you. Oh, that we could get at the thousands in London that do not know it, the multitudes that never enter a house of prayer or yield attention to the gospel message. Our heart yearns over them, but what more can we do for them? They are perishing in willful ignorance. Thanks be to God that so many are here today; I will seize the opportunity to declare the plan of grace. Though so many of you know it, let us tell it to you again. By sin, by unrighteousness, by violation of God's law, we have broken our peace with God. We are lost, for he must punish sin. It is not possible that he should be the righteous governor of the universe and allow sin to go unpunished. To punish sin is no arbitrary purpose of an angry God. It is inevitable in the universe that where there is evil there should be suffering. If not in this life yet in another life, which will shortly succeed that which now is, every transgression must receive its proper

> It is not possible that God should be the righteous governor of the universe and allow sin to go unpunished.

recompense of reward. The question is, How can we be forgiven? How, consistently with divine justice, can our iniquities be blotted out? This is not a profound problem left for us to work out; God's way of peace is made clear by revelation.

God, in his infallible Word, has told us the means and tools by which guilty sinners can be made righteous before him, and, instead of being driven from his presence at the last, may be accepted and dwell at his right hand. He tells us that inasmuch as the first sin that ruined us was not ours but Adam's, and by the transgression of one man we all fell, so it became possible for him, in consistency with justice, to ordain that another man should be forthcoming in whom we may rise and be restored. That other man has come – "the second Adam, the Lord from heaven." But the task of lifting up was much harder than that of casting down. A mere man could ruin us, but a mere man could not redeem and rescue us.

Therefore, God himself, the ever-blessed, clothed himself with the nature of man, was born of a woman, lay in Bethlehem's manger, lived here on earth a life of humiliation and self-denial, and at the last took upon himself the sins of men in one vast load. Even as the fabled Atlas was said to carry the world upon his shoulders, so Jesus took sin and guilt upon him and bore it in his own body on the tree. On the cross Jesus hung as the substitute for all of our race that ever will believe on him, and there and then he put away by his suffering all the transgression and iniquity of believing men, so that now we can preach to mankind and say, *"Whoever believes in Him shall not perish." "He who believes in the Son has eternal life."*

When you go to a foreign city for the first time and stay at an inn, it may be that you miss your way when you go out, and are not able to get back again as easily as you wish. It is generally expedient, therefore, for travelers to learn the main streets of every town which they visit. In Rome we come to know which way the Corso runs, and when we get an idea of the run of that main thoroughfare, we by and by are able to pick our way through the city. Now, the main street of the gospel is *substitution. He made Him who knew no sin to be sin on our behalf, so that we might become the righteousness of God in Him.* The main street of the gospel runs crosswise; follow it, and you will know the ins and outs of the other great streets before long. This is the High Street of the City of Grace – *Christ redeemed us from the curse of the Law, having become a curse for us.* Christ stood in our stead, and suffered that we might not suffer. He *died . . . the just for the unjust, so that He might bring us to God.* Whosoever believes in Christ is saved from the damning power of sin and delivered from the wrath to come.

Take this fact in all its breadth and length, and never doubt it, and you have the key to the gospel. Whosoever, I say, trusts his soul with the Lord Jesus Christ, relying on that sacrifice which he offered, and that death which he endured, is saved. Let him not doubt it. He has God's word for it; let him believe it and rejoice in it. *"He who believes in Him is not judged,"* for, *"as Moses lifted up the serpent in the wilderness, even so must the Son of Man be lifted up; so that whoever believes will in Him have eternal life."* Simple, childlike reliance upon the Lord Jesus gives immediate and complete salvation to the trustful soul.

Well, that is the main street of the city. Now, how to get into it is the question; and I earnestly desire, and devoutly hope, to be the means, if God will help me, of leading some thereto. May the Holy Spirit now bear witness with the truth, and make it the power of God unto salvation. Our text says, *"Take courage, stand up! He is calling for you."*

Our first point is that *some who are seeking Christ greatly want comforting.* Secondly, *their very best comfort lies in the fact that Jesus calls them.* But, thirdly, *if they take the comfort of that call, it urges them to immediate action* – *"Stand up!"* *"Take courage, stand up! He is calling for you."*

First, then, many persons who are really seeking the Savior greatly want comforting.

I know there are many such here today. You long for everlasting life. God has worked in you a desire to be reconciled to himself; but you need encouraging, for *you labor under a sort of undefined fear that these good things are not for you.* Partly your conscience, partly your unbelief, and partly Satan – these three have joined together to throw a mist over you, and you really think that you cannot be forgiven. You would not like to put it into exactly those words, but such is the tendency of your thoughts. There is a hazy idea about you that there are many very good saintly people who will be saved, and, indeed, that there are some great transgressors who will be saved; but you do not think that *you* can be.

Oh, that I could destroy that unbelieving thought! There is salvation, there is mercy, there is forgiveness, and all are free to every soul that will come and take them. They are as free as the air you breathe, or as the water leaping from the street fountain yonder. *Let the one who wishes take of the water of life without cost.* You are mistaken in those gloomy reflections. You write bitter things against yourself, but God has not written them. What if you should take heart and get a hope, thinking, "Perhaps I may today find eternal life. Perhaps I may today go out of this house relieved of the burden of my sin." It would be a good beginning if you had such a hope, but you may with confidence go a great deal further.

It may be that *you are cast down because you think that you have been seeking in vain.* You began to pray a few months ago, young man, and I am glad to hear of it; but you have not yet obtained peace. Do not give up praying. I know you are discouraged, but do not cease seeking. I myself was for many months an earnest seeker after God by the way of prayer. I thought that by compelling prayer I should find pardon. I did not understand that he had said, *"Believe in the Lord Jesus, and you will be saved."* So I set to work praying. Nevertheless, I am thankful that I did not cease from prayer, though it often seemed as if I wasted my words and spent my tears for nothing. Be not discouraged. This blind man was not heard at first, though he cried earnestly. He had to cry for sight again and again, increasing in vehemence each time. Do not be driven to despair. There may be delays, but there shall never be denials to those who cry in earnest. Be of good comfort. Press on, dear heart, press on, and you shall find peace and comfort yet.

Perhaps, too, you are sad *because there are many round about you who discourage you.* They tell you there is nothing in religion. How would they know? Theirs is a strange infatuation. There are a great many individuals in the world who are considered to be honest in business; you would take their promissory note, and you would trust their word about any goods they were selling. Yet when these good folks begin to say that they are conscious of a new life within them – that they have found out that God is real and spiritual, and that they have received a

Spirit which dwells within them, or that they commune with God, right away a number of people say that it is not true – in effect calling them liars. And why not true? On what grounds are they to be discredited?

Simply because the forenamed people who deny it say that they never saw such a thing themselves and never felt such a thing themselves. But if there was a world full of blind people, and among them a few persons blessed with sight, whose eyes had been opened, if these began to talk of sunlight and color, all the blind men might say, "It is not true." Why? "Because *we* never saw the sunlight or the color." Does that prove that it is not true? Though *you* do not possess the faculties of vision, others do. If those men are honest in other things, they have as much right to be believed in this thing as in the rest.

We solemnly assert that there is something real in religion. It is not a creed alone, it is a life. The regenerate belong to a new creation. If any man be in Christ he is a new creature with new faculties and new powers, so that he is introduced altogether into a new world. Do not believe those, then, who tell you that there is nothing in it, for they do not know, and therefore they are not fair witnesses. They can witness to nothing but the fact that they are not in the secret. The man who was brought up for a murder which was sworn against him by six witnesses said that he ought not to be condemned because he could bring sixty witnesses who did not see him do it. Of course he could; and so can we bring sixty thousand people to say there is no spiritual life because *they* have never felt it. What does that prove? It only proves that they know nothing about it. But if you bring a few – even though they should be but a few – straightforward, honest, simple-minded people whom you would believe in other things, you are bound to accept their testimony about this. There is something real in faith in Jesus. There is a peace which passes all understanding obtained through pardoned sin. There is a new birth, for we have felt it; there is a new life, for we enjoy it. There is a joy that overleaps earth's narrow bounds. There is a rest of heart akin to the rest of the blessed in heaven, and it can be enjoyed here and now; thousands of us bear witness that it is so.

Do not be discouraged then, for we tell you no old wives' fables, but the very truth which we have ourselves tasted and handled. You that

> **If any man be in Christ he is a new creature.**

are seeking after eternal life need not be baffled by skeptics; we are true men, and we tell you what we have proved for ourselves. You will yet find it to be as God declares.

One reason why you have not obtained comfort is, perhaps, *because you do not know all the gospel yet.* Good news half told may often seem to be bad news. I have read that in the days of the semaphore signals a message came across to England concerning the Duke of Wellington, and half the message was read as it appeared upon the semaphore, and astonished all England with the sad intelligence. It ran thus: "Wellington defeated." Everybody was distressed as they read it, but it so happened that they had not seen the whole message. Fog had intervened, and when, by and by, the air was clearer and the telegraph flashed out a second time, it was read thus – "Wellington defeated *the French*" – quite another thing, quite the reverse indeed of what half the message had led men to fear.

Thus when you hear half the gospel it may appear to condemn you; but you have only to hear the other half to find out its encouraging tidings. I would say, be diligent in hearing the gospel; be diligent in searching it out in the sacred book which God has given to us; and when you know the truth more fully you will find faith come to you by the hearing and the understanding of the Word of God. Leave those ministers who preach only a portion of the gospel, and try to know all the message of love, and you will, by the teaching of the Holy Spirit, soon lose your fears.

Do you not think, too, that some seekers miss comfort because *they forget that Jesus Christ is alive*? The Christ of the Church of Rome is always seen in one of two positions – either as a babe in his mother's arms, or else as dead. That is Rome's Christ, but our Christ is alive. Jesus who rose has "left the dead no more to die." I was requested in Turin to join with others in asking to see the shroud in which the Savior was buried. I must confess that I had not faith enough to believe in the shroud, nor had I curiosity enough to wish to look at the fictitious linen. I would not care a penny for the article, even if I knew it to be genuine. Our Lord has left his shroud and sepulcher, and he lives in heaven. Today, he so lives that a sigh of yours will reach him; a tear will find him; a desire in your heart will bring him to you. Only seek him as a loving, living

Savior, and put your trust in him as risen from the dead no more to die, and comfort will, I trust, come into your spirit.

Perhaps, too, *you have a notion that conversion is something very terrible.* A young woman came to me the other day, after a service, to ask me whether I really meant what I said when I declared that he that believed in Jesus Christ was saved there and then. "Yes," I said; and I gave her the scriptural warrant for it. "Why," she said, "my grandfather told me that when he found religion it took him six months, and they had nearly to put him into a lunatic asylum. He was in such a dreadful state of mind." "Well, well," I said, "that sometimes happens. But that distress of his did not save him. That was simply his conscience and Satan together keeping him away from Christ. When he was saved it was not by his deep feelings; it was by his believing in Jesus Christ." I then went on to set Christ before her as our sole ground of hope in opposition to inward feelings. "I *see* it," she said; and I rejoiced as I noticed the bright light that passed over her face, a flash of heavenly sunlight which I have often seen on the countenances of those who have believed in Jesus Christ, when peace fills the soul even to the brim, and lights up the countenance with a minor transfiguration. It is so. You have but to trust Christ, and it is done. But you are afraid.

Have you never heard of the man who lost his way one night, and came to the edge of a precipice, as he thought, and fell over, and clutched at some old tree, and there hung, clinging to his frail support with all his might, for he felt that he should be dashed to pieces if he fell? There he hung till he got into a desperate state of fever, and his hands could hold up his body no longer; so at last he dropped and fell – about half a dozen inches – onto a smooth mossy bank, on which he lay, altogether unhurt, and quite safe. Now, there are many who think that sure destruction must await them if they confess sin and resign all into the hands of God. It is an idle fear. Give up your hold upon everything but Christ, and drop down. Soft and mossy shall the bank be which receives you. Jesus Christ, by his love and by the effectualness of his precious blood, shall give you immediate rest and peace. Only drop now. Drop down at once; this is the major part of faith – the giving up of every other hold, and simply falling upon Christ. That dropping-down will bring you present salvation.

Now, in the second place, the greatest comfort which I can very well conceive is that which is conveyed in the text. It is this – *"Take courage, stand up! He is calling for you"* – a good word for the blind man, for he knew that Jesus did not call him to mock him, and that he did not say, "Come here," so that he might merely tell him, "Your eyes cannot be opened." Jesus did not call him to sport with him and send him away disappointed. Christ's calls are honest calls and they guarantee blessing to those who accept them.

Now, beloved friends, there are two calls mentioned in Scripture. The one is the *general call* of the gospel, and the other is the *effectual call,* the personal call, by which men are saved.

The general universal call ought to yield great comfort to any seeking soul. In the Word of God, *you,* dear hearer, are called to come to Christ, even *you.* Why do I know that? Because when Jesus gave the commission to his disciples, he said, *"Go into all the world and preach the gospel to all creation."* You are one of his *"all creation,"* are you not? Well, then, you must be included in that range. We are to preach the gospel *to you.* And then again, *It is a trustworthy statement, deserving full acceptance, that Christ Jesus came into the world to save sinners.* You are a sinner, are you not? Do you not admit that? Very well, then, according to the text, that faithful saying is to be addressed to you.

And you, dear seeker, feel a burden upon your soul, do you not? You are laboring hard to get salvation. Therefore, the gospel call must be addressed to you. *"Come to Me, all who are weary and heavy-laden, and I will give you rest."* Indeed there are many such calls, but there is another which must include you – *Let the one who wishes take the water of life without cost.* Are you willing to come? Then you are undoubtedly called to come to Christ. Should not that fact comfort you? Because, as I have already said, he does not call you to mock you, or invite you to come without intending to bless you. Oh, hear his honest call, and pluck up courage and come to him. Nobody feels any trouble about going where there is a general invitation.

Did you ever cross the Mount St. Bernard? If so, I do not suppose you lacked any pressing feeling to turn into the inn there and spend the night. When they came out and told you that everybody was welcome, rich and poor, and that nearly all travelers stayed there, you turned in. I went the other day to St. Cross Hospital, near Winchester, which some of you may know. There they give away a piece of bread to everybody who knocks at the door. I knocked as bold as brass. Why should I not? If they gave the bread away to everybody, why should I not have my piece? And so, of course, the hatch was opened, and I had my little piece of bread with the friends who were with me. It was an allotted share to be given to everybody that called. I did not humble myself particularly and make anything special of it; it was for all, and I came and received as one of the people who were willing to knock.

Now, even so, if the gospel is to be preached to every creature, why stand you haggling when you want the Bread of Life? Why should you waste time in raising question after question when you only need to take what Jesus freely gives? I will bet that you do not raise such quibbles against yourselves in money matters. If an estate is bequeathed you, you do not employ a solicitor to hunt for flaws in the title, or to invent objections to the will. Why do men raise difficulties against their own salvation, instead of cheerfully accepting what the infinite mercy of God so graciously provides for all who with broken hearts and willing minds are ready to take what God, the ever-bountiful, is so pleased to give?

The invitation is so large, and there is this to be noted concerning it: *No one has ever been refused.* There is a well-known institution in London which bears across the front of it: "No destitute boy ever refused." Well may we put this over Christ's great house of mercy – "No destitute soul ever refused." I can imagine two boys standing on the pavement in front of Dr. Barnardo's institution, and one saying to the other, "Can *we* go in there?" "Yes," says the other, "I should rather think we could. We are destitute, aren't we? Look here, my clothes are all in rags, and I have not a penny in the world, and no father and no mother. I slept under a dry arch last night. I am a destitute boy, and no mistake."

I can only suppose that the other might boastfully say, "I ain't destitute; not I. I can earn my living any day, and I have a half-crown in my pocket." Now, that fellow has no claim to be admitted because he is not destitute; but the boy who is hungry and ragged and homeless is sure to be welcomed. As he reads those lines, "No destitute boy ever refused," he says, "There is hope for me then." Now then, destitute soul, Jesus Christ never refused one like you. If you have a store of merit of your own, if you believe you can be saved by your good works, you do not come under the heading of "destitute." *"It is not those who are healthy who need a physician, but those who are sick."* But if you are stripped of all boasting, if you are brought to bankruptcy as to personal merit, if you have come down to absolute poverty as to any hope in yourself, then, as no destitute soul ever was rejected or ever shall be, come to Jesus at once! Come at once, I say. *"Take courage, stand up! He is calling for you."*

But, dear friends, I said that there was another and *an effectual call.* That call the Holy Spirit directs to individuals, and when it comes, it is not resisted, or if resisted for a while, it is ultimately yielded to, so that the man is constrained to come. O Holy Spirit, give that call today. There were two brothers fishing, and Jesus said to them, *"Follow Me."* They threw down their nets and followed him. Matthew was sitting at the receipt of customs, with his pen behind his ear and his account books before him. Jesus said, *"Follow Me!"* Up rose Matthew, and followed him at once. That little fellow, the tax gatherer, had climbed up a tree because, being short of stature, he could not see over the heads of the crowd. While he was looking down from among the leafy branches, the Master stood at the bottom of the tree and said, *"Zaccheus, hurry and come down, for today I must stay at your house."* Down came Zaccheus. How could he help it? The Spirit of God had given the effectual call, and Christ was in that man's house shortly after, and the man gave abundant evidence of a change of heart. Oh, may the eternal Spirit speak in that fashion to some present here, so that they may at once yield and follow Jesus Christ.

That call, wherever it comes, *casts a sweet softness over the soul.* The man cannot make it out, but he feels so differently from what he did before. The iron sinew of his neck is gone. The cold stone within his breast has melted into flesh. He listens to the gospel which once he despised. Listening, he thinks; and it is a grand matter to get a man to think about himself, his God, eternity, heaven, hell, and the Redeemer. As he thinks, he sees his life in a different light. He perceives that there has been sin in it – much more sin than he ever thought could have been there; and, as he sees his sin, he mourns over it. He almost wishes that he had never been born rather than have transgressed as he has done. His heart softens down under the influence of the law of God. He lays aside his proud boastings, and confesses that he is full of transgression and sin. Next to this thoughtfulness and repentance comes a little hope; he perceives that there is a salvation worth having, and he asks himself why he should not have it. Then comes faith; he perceives that Jesus is the Son of God, and he says to himself, "If he is divine, he can save even me." He trusts, and as he trusts, the darkness which enveloped him begins to disappear. He obtains a little light, and yet a little more, and at last he cries, "I do believe that Jesus died for me. I rest my soul in his pierced hands. I am forgiven – I am saved." That man has been called by the blessed Spirit.

It is very strange, too, how God calls some men. I have known it to happen many times in this tabernacle. I have been preaching and I have made a remark which has suited the case as well as if I had been that man's companion, or better. How was it? I will tell you, God had been at work on that man, and he led his servant to work to the same point. The Lord was by his providence tunneling one side of the mountain of the man's indifference, and then he set me to work on the other side by guiding me in my thoughts so that I preached the gospel in a suitable manner.

Just as when they made the Mont Cenis Tunnel, one set of engineers was boring one way and one set the other way, and then they met in the heart of the great mountain. A devoted mother has been boring away at the mountain by her pleadings, or an earnest Christian teacher, or a wife, or a sister has been at the same work. Perhaps sickness, like the diamond-boring rod, has been piercing into the man, and then at last in this place the word of the Lord has exactly hit the case, so that the tunnel through the soul has been completed, and eternal salvation has been the result. Perhaps the chance words of this night are no chance words to some of you now present, but are the very words of God sent straight to your soul. God grant that it may be so, and he shall have the praise. O eternal Spirit, thus let it be.

Now, lest I weary you, I am going to close with the third topic, which is that the comfort drawn from our calling should lead to immediate action. *"Take courage, stand up! He is calling for you."*

That exhortation to stand up means instant *decision.* You have been hesitating and hanging like the scales of a balance, trembling between heaven and hell. Which is it to be? May the Holy Spirit call you so that it shall be Christ, salvation, and eternal life. I am not always sorry when men grow angry while hearing a sermon. The worst thing that can happen to me today is for you all to be satisfied. But when some people get very angry they will think, and thinking they will feel, and feeling they may turn to God. Despite their anger they will come again. The hook is in the man's jaws. We shall have that fish. Let him draw out the line further and further, for it will hold him. Let him play. We shall have him back again before long. Have the landing net ready! There is nothing better for some men than to have their antagonism to the gospel aroused for a time. The truth has come home to them. It is at work on them, and, before long, we trust the blessed work will be complete, and the soul will be saved. This is the point aimed at.

"Stand up!" says the text. That is, do not let it be any longer a question of "Shall it be?" or "Shall it not be?" but decide today – *"It shall be.* By the grace of God I will be a Christian. By the grace of God, if there is salvation to be had, I will have it." I do not ask you to come to that decision for the mere sake of making a resolution, which you will cordially adopt and then carelessly forget, but I do ask the grace of God to lead you to say with purpose of heart, "It shall be." Alas, very many of you come and go; you hear and hear without profit, for it ends in hearing and never ripens into decision. Too many of our regular hearers still remain unconverted though occasional hearers have been saved. When you take hold of a piece of India rubber, you may make any impression that you like all over it, but in the end it resumes its old shape. There are hosts of hearers of that kind: very capable of being impressed, but they quickly return to their old tastes and habits.

But you meet with other people who seem to be as hard as flint. I have observed some who have sat in the aisle biting their lips, who have never intended to believe the gospel, and yet with one blow of the Master's hammer their hearts have gone to shivers directly. Their armor of resistance and their armor plates of defiance have been broken through, and they have proved afterwards the heartiest and most earnest of Christian converts. That is an unfortunate impressibility which ends in indecision. Those who show this plastic character mean to be right, but they manage to remain in the wrong. They intend to go to heaven, but, alas, little hope is there that they will ever reach the city of the blessed. The probabilities are against it. They have passed so many years in procrastination that their indecision has become chronic, and binds them to their sins. After the many seasons in which fair leaves have disappointed the hope of sweet fruits, our despondency is, we fear, the herald of their despair. There seems so little probability that they will ever decide for God and for his Christ, that we scarcely hope with trembling; no, we rather tremble to hope. I wish to God it were not so.

Oh, dear friends! I pray you listen to the text. *"Take courage, stand up! He is calling for you."* Rise to something more than decision: rise to *resolution*. You have all heard of the poor woman who could not get justice done for her by the judge. She called on him a great many times, but he would not hearken to her. At length she made up her mind that he *should* attend to her; so she was present on the first court day, and as soon as the judge came in she rose and said, "My lord." "Have I not told you not to trouble me?" he said. "But my lord," she cried again. "I tell you to sit down," he said. She sits down, but before the court is up, she says, "Can't I have a hearing?" "I cannot attend, to you now, my good woman," he says. But when the judge comes out of court to go home, there she is standing at the carriage window, saying, "When will you hear my case? There are my poor children starving." She goes to the house and knocks at untimely hours. "Who is it?" the judge asks; and they tell him, "It is that poor woman who wants her case to be heard." He bids them to chase her from his gate. She goes home, sad but determined, and the next morning she is in court again. The unjust judge had commanded the ushers not to let her in, but she has entered somehow, and the first thing that is heard is that shrill voice – "My lord, will you hear me?" At last he grows tired, and he says, *"Though I fear not God, nor regard man; Yet because this widow troubleth me, I will avenge her, lest by her continual coming she weary me"* (KJV). And he does avenge her.

Though the just God bears no resemblance to an unjust judge, yet the widow's urgency that prevailed in the teeth of such unpromising surroundings may urge you to incessant prayer. Treat the great God with the urgency which Christ by so bold a simile counsels and commends. Say thus to yourself: "I cannot perish. I must perish if I do not have salvation; and therefore I will have it. I will die at the foot of the cross if die I must, but I will have it."

It happened to me some few years ago that I had to lecture at the Glasgow City Hall. I went at the hour appointed to keep my engagement, and the provost of Glasgow went to the hall with me, but the policeman said that he could not let us in, for we had no tickets, and his orders were to admit none without them. That was a pretty state of things. So the lord provost said, "But you must let us in." The policeman said that he could not, no matter who we were. I said, "This is the lord provost." But the policeman said he did not know that, neither did he care who he was; he would not let us pass against rules. He had received orders from the inspector to let nobody in, and he was sure no lord provost would wish him to disobey orders. Then the lord provost said, "But this is Mr. Spurgeon. He has got to deliver the lecture." The policeman responded, "I cannot help that. I have my orders, and he shall not come in without a ticket." What do you think we did? Did we take "No" for an answer? Not so. We meant to get in. So we talked and parleyed and reasoned; but he, like a good policeman, did his duty, and would take no commands from us which were contrary to orders. There we stopped. At last he was condescending enough to let us send our cards in to his inspector, and immediately we were admitted. Now, if we had taken "No" for an answer, and had gone away, I would have had to this day the reputation of having gathered the people together to disappoint them. No, I knew I had a right to go in, and I meant to get in, and I did get in. You must do the same.

Even though your sin should prohibit you, and the law should denounce you, and the officer of justice should refuse you and say, "You cannot come in; no sinner comes this way," yet insist upon it that you are a creature and a sinner – that the gospel is sent to every creature, and especially invites sinners, and therefore you mean to go in to the feast of grace, whoever may oppose. Stand to it that you will enter, and as surely as God is true, if there be this resolve and perseverance in you, you shall enter into the banquet of love, you shall inherit eternal life, and rejoice forevermore.

But, dear friends, if you get to that decision and resolution, there is one thing more, and that is, *cast away everything that hinders you from finding salvation.* The poor blind man cast away his garment. Now, if you would be saved, you must resolve in your soul, by the blessing of the Holy Spirit, that every sin and every habit of yours which hinders your finding Christ at once shall be given up. There is no pleasure worth keeping at the price of your soul. No sin is worth preserving on any account whatever; let all your old pleasures and habits go, let them all go, and give yourself up to Jesus Christ. How I wish that many today might be led to say, "There is salvation then for me by believing. I believe that the Word of God is true, and I take Christ to be mine." Do give yourselves up wholly to Christ. No half measures; no hesitating and faltering now.

You know what Cortez did when he went to Mexico and intended to conquer it. The soldiers that were with him were few and dispirited. The Mexicans were many, and the enterprise hazardous. The soldiers would have gone back to Spain, but Cortez took two or three chosen heroes with him, and went down to the seaside and broke up all the ships. "Now," he said, "we must conquer or die. We cannot go back." Burn your boats; get rid of all thoughts of return; leave sin, and abhor it. God help you to do so, for this is his gospel – "Repent and be converted, every one of you." Forsake sin and believe in Jesus Christ, and let the boats be burned, making this your resolution – that there shall be no going back to sin anymore.

> We can set the plan of salvation before men, but we cannot induce them to accept it, unless the eternal Spirit moves in the souls of men.

Thus have I told you what should be done, but God alone can make you do it. We can lead a horse to the water, but we cannot make him drink; so we can set the plan of salvation before men, but we cannot induce them to accept it, unless, in answer to prayer, the eternal Spirit moves in the souls of men. He is moving upon you now. We are conscious that he is brooding over some of you at this hour. Resist him not. Yield yourselves wholly to his admonitions. As the bulrushes in the stream bow their heads to the passing breeze, so bow before the motions of the ever-blessed Spirit. May he help you to do so, for Jesus' sake. Amen.

Chapter 5

The Soul's Crisis

Jesus of Nazareth was passing by. (Luke 18:37)

Such was the news of that day. As an exclamation, doubtless it was often repeated when our Lord made his journeys through the land of Palestine and its outskirts – "Jesus of Nazareth is passing by!" How quickly would the inhabitants of their cities and their villages be abuzz when the rumor reached them! What a curiosity there would be to see him, knowing that his fame was reported abroad everywhere! What an eagerness among the multitudes to get close enough to hear him! What an intense anxiety on the part of some to go themselves, and of others to take their sick and diseased friends that they might obtain health and a cure! Oh, I think there was enough in those words to make men forego awhile their farms and their merchandise, their labors and their pleasures, that they might feast their eyes and ears on the sight of his face and the sound of his voice – or much more, that they might obtain some grateful relief and get some substantial benefit from him who went about doing good.

But, my dear brethren, I want you to catch the spiritual significance of these thrilling words. If you understood them correctly, you would rise up and shake off your lethargy. You would be eager to greet his presence, and anxious to learn his doctrine. That, however, which I am sure would stir you to the heart's core and excite all your passions is the vehement desire to have salvation, present salvation, from him. Surely you would be ready to receive him into your house, to welcome him into your heart, and to sit at his feet dissolved in wonder, love, and praise. And yet very many of you who join the throng and mingle with the families that come up to seek the Lord are as unconcerned for yourselves as though your sins were of no weight, and your souls in no immediate peril.

Oh, it is high time that some here present were saved. In a short time you might be in another world. Close to that column, on my right in yonder gallery, in that next pew, there have usually sat two attentive hearers, husband and wife, who early this morning were suffocated by the smoke of their own burning house, just under these eaves. I little thought that they would be preachers to us today – but they are so. The calamity, sudden and mysterious, which has removed them from our midst, sets the uncertainty of life and the preparation for departure so vividly before us that we cannot refrain our emotions or restrain our sympathies. Their absence should speak loudly to those who occupy the seats they have vacated, asking them whether they are ready to depart. Not less loudly should it speak to all sitting here, raising the question in the hearts of some of you who are careless about your souls, how you could bear to pass out of this world if the arrow of death should overtake you unawares. A trifling accident may prove fatal, a slight illness may be the precursor of speedy disintegration.

Can you imagine your own remorse as you glance backwards at the gospel you have listened to but never embraced – the blood of sprinkling you have heard of but has never been applied to your conscience – the Savior whom you passed by with indifference when he passed by you, ready to be gracious, and you would not be his disciple? Ah! you may turn from such questions with a faint smile now, but before long you will turn to them with a pale shudder.

Are there any here present who are anxious to be saved? Let me have their solemn, earnest, and devout attention. I pray God that what I speak simply may just strike their consciences and touch their hearts. If they want their judgments informed, may the Word come with light to their spirits, and in that light may they behold Christ and find salvation.

Our text is taken from a little narrative of a blind man who sat by the highway side begging – not an inept picture of you, my friends, who are thoughtful of mercy, and anxiously desirous of salvation. Are you not as blind and poor spiritually as he was literally? I am sure that you will at once confess that you are blind. The eyes of your understanding are dim; your heart is wrapped in darkness. You cannot see what you want to see. You do not even see your sin so as to repent of it with contrition. You have not yet seen the power of the precious blood of Jesus so as to believe in it as worshipers once purged and abundantly conscious that it has procured their remission.

While you are as blind, I am quite sure that you will not be grieved or vexed with me if I say, too, that you are as poor as Bartimaeus. His was poverty of pennies, but yours is poverty of soul. You have no merit; you have no strength; you have no possibility of ever getting the means of spiritual livelihood for yourselves. You are as poor as the poorest beggar that ever asked for alms for God's sake from the wanderers. But you are sitting today in somewhat the same position as that blind man was, for he sat in the place of Jesus' passing by, and you have come to the place where God's mercy has often been revealed, where saints and sinners have passed by in crowds, and where – blessed be his name! – Jesus himself sometimes has also passed by.

What if today you should be apprised and aware of his presence here, and should cry out to him, and he should stop and open those blind eyes of yours, and give you the light of life and the joy of eternal salvation? What if you should have to go home and say to your friends and relatives, "I have had an experience today the like of which I never felt before. I have found a Savior, I have received the forgiveness of my sins, and I am a new creature in Christ Jesus"? Why, you would make angels sing fresh hallelujahs in heaven, while on earth God would be glorified, and yourselves and your friends would be blessed by so lively an exercise of faith and so wonderful a participation of grace.

Now, looking steadfastly that this may be the case, I wish to speak very pointedly to you about two or three things. First, when Jesus passed by the blind man it was to that man a day of hope.

He had given up all thought of ever being able to see, so long had his eyes been closed to the light. When Jesus passed by, the case was different. He could perform any miracle, there was no limit to his healing power; therefore, why should he not open a blind man's eyes? And you, my anxious friend, you have felt that you could not be saved. Of course, if it depended upon yourself, you could not by any duties you discharged, or any services you performed, acquire merit enough to enter heaven, or even to procure the forgiveness of your sins on earth. But, if Jesus Christ has come into the world to save that which was lost, it is a totally different matter. He can certainly pardon the greatest offenders, and he can deliver from going down into the pit the most undeserving of rebels. It was an hour of hope to that blind man, and if Jesus passes by now, this is an hour of hope to you.

But, does he pass by? I answer – Yes. There are different respects in which this may be interpreted of our Lord's conduct. In a certain sense he has been passing by some of you ever since you began to discern right from wrong. You have, some of you, been nurtured and brought up under the hearing of the gospel, and you cannot recollect the time when you did not know something, at any rate, of the facts and truths that pertain to Christianity. Well, all this while Jesus Christ has been slowly passing by you – halting, pausing, giving you space if perhaps you would call to him for mercy. O take heed, that passing by may soon be over; the candle of life may be blown out. Yet while the gospel rings in your ears, it is a day of hope to you. Let not Satan or your own despairing heart persuade you to the contrary.

More especially is it a time of Christ's passing by *when the gospel is preached with power.* If today the gospel should so come to you as to win your attention and melt your heart, if you should feel a divine control exerted over you by it, then the evidence will not be lacking that Jesus is passing by. Or, if the gospel, though it does not affect you, should convey such an influence, and bring forth such fruits in others who are sitting in the same pew with you that they should be saved, then depend upon it that the kingdom of God will have come near unto you. It will then have passed by and you will have received no blessing because you did not seek it in faith. Yet responsibilities will have come upon you from which you will not be able to escape. Jesus will have passed by other blind men; they will have asked for sight, and received it, while you will remain blind, not because Jesus cannot heal you, but because you have not asked for his healing, but have continued still in your unbelief of him.

I feel conscious within myself that this very night Jesus is, in a special manner, present in this assembly. Sometimes the preacher has yearnings within himself for the people as if he labored in birth until Christ be formed in them. He wrestles with such an earnest longing after souls as if their peril and the conflict for their rescue were all his own; that is no slight omen of the coming blessing. He perceives, also, the same desire in many of his converted hearers. As he knows that they are praying to God with much vehemence of spirit to bring in the sinner, the atmosphere of prayer becomes to him an indication of the time and the place where Jesus manifests himself; for where his people pray, Christ is surely present. I encourage you then with hopeful signs of heavenly grace. This is a hopeful hour. If you have lived up till now unsaved, I indulge the fervent hope that the hour has now come when you shall find salvation. Though you may up to this time have sought, and sought, and sought in vain, yet now surely the set time to favor you has come. Lord, grant it may be so, that it may be so to many, and we will bless your name.

> A man cannot be saved by what he does; salvation is in Christ, yet no man is saved unless he seeks earnestly after Christ.

Secondly, as it was a time of hope for that poor blind man, so was it especially a time of activity.

You who anxiously desire salvation, regard attentively these words. A man cannot be saved by what he does; salvation is in Christ, yet no man is saved unless he seeks earnestly after Christ. This blind man did not open his eyes himself. What he did, did not help or contribute in any degree to his attaining sight. Nevertheless, he had to seek Jesus to have his eyes opened. There was enough in this to kindle all his passions, summon all his faculties, and engage all his energies; but most certainly there was nothing in it to exercise his skill in discovering or applying a remedy, nothing to win him any honor, and nothing to entitle him to any reward.

Yet this man is a picture of what we should be if we desire to be saved. *He listened attentively.* He could not see, but he had ears. He could catch the sound of footsteps. The silence that was broken by crowds coming along the road to Jericho was peculiar, the tramp was of an unusual sort, and the tone of voices far different from those of wrangling or of revelry, or the songs of common travelers. He listened, yes, he listened with all his ears. So, whenever the gospel is preached, do not give it merely such a hearing as you might give to an ordinary story that is told to you. But oh, hear it as God's word, hear it with bated breath and profound reverence; drink it in as the parched earth drinks in the shower; hear it fearing to miss a single word, lest that should be the word that might have blessed you. I believe attentive hearers are the most likely people to get the blessing. Let none of us, therefore, when we go to the courts of the Lord's house and hear a gospel sermon, permit our thoughts to be wandering here and there, but let us give scrupulous heed, if so be it that we may detect the footsteps of the Lord by the conversation of his disciples.

But this man, after he had heard with discrimination, *inquired with eagerness what it meant.* Oh! how I wish our hearers would begin to ask, "What does it mean?" I can say that I put my words as plainly as I can. Oftentimes when there is a bunch of gaudy flowers of rhetoric that I would rather use, and could use, I have thrown them all on the dunghill, because they might have stood in some poor sinner's way, and he might not have understood the plain truth so well. Ah! but still, for all that, talk as we may, the carnal mind understands not the things that are of God. It is a blessed sign when men begin to say, "What is it all about? What is the drift of this gospel? What does the man mean by sin and its heinousness? What does he mean by Christ and his precious blood? What is it all about?"

> Whenever the gospel is preached, hear it as God's word, hear it with profound reverence.

Some of you only skim your Bibles when you read them. I wish you would stop and ponder, and ask of Christian people who have experienced these things, "What do these texts mean?" So too, if there be anything in a sermon that baffles you, I wish you would seek out some godly and instructed Christian, and say, "Explain to me, father, what this thing signifies." I should have great hopes of you if you were thus inquiring after the plan of salvation. Is it not worth your while to ask the question, sirs? When a man has lost his way, he will ask twenty people sooner than he will continue to pursue a wrong course, and will you lose your way to heaven through not asking old travelers to direct you? Do, I pray you, be in earnest to learn, and it shall not be long before God shall teach you, for whenever he makes a man conscious of his ignorance, and anxious to be taught, God the Holy Spirit is quite sure to instruct him before long.

When this man had asked the question, and had been told in reply that Jesus of Nazareth was passing by, notice what he did next: *he began to pray.* We are told that he cried. His cry was a prayer, and his prayer was a cry. It took the form of a pitiful and emphatic outburst of desire: *"Jesus, Son of David, have mercy on me!"* It was a short prayer. He did not need a prayer book. Being a blind man he could not have used one if he had had it. Blessed be God, we need no book of prayers. We need such prayers as blind men can use quite as readily as those who can see. And what a comprehensive prayer it was – *"Have mercy on me!" "Have mercy on me!"* It was not the *words* of the prayer, it was the true desire and the believing confidence of the prayer that did the work. *"Jesus, Son of David, have mercy on me!"*

Now, my dear hearer, you tell me that you wish to be saved, that you are anxious, no, inquiring; but do you pray? How can you expect mercy if it is not thought by you to be worth the asking for? What, will you have God give you it without your seeking it? He has done so sometimes, but the usual rule of grace, and the most proper rule, is that you should humbly plead for mercy at his feet. Will you not do it? What! Is hell so despicable a doom that you will not pray to escape from it? What! Is heaven so trifling a destination that you will not pray that you may gain it?

O sirs, when heavenly mercy is to be had for the asking, will you not invoke the Almighty, and do homage to the Redeemer to obtain it? Then how richly you deserve to die! Being placed on pleading terms, you will not plead, and being bidden to seek the Lord while he may be found, you willfully refuse to seek him! Yes, richly do you deserve to perish in your sin! But it must not be so with you. I cannot look you in the face and think you will do such disdain to God's claims and your own interests. No, you will pray, I trust you will; you will cry with your whole heart to God. Be assured that never did a man really cry for mercy, and continue to do so with his whole heart, but sooner or later mercy came. There are no praying souls in hell. God never damns those who are pleaders for mercy. If you do but lay hold on the cross of Christ and say, "I will not let this go unless I get the blessing; I will not cease until I win my soul's desire," then you shall soon have the mercy that you seek. O that God would stir you up thus to pray!

As this man prayed, there were some standing by who said, "Hush, hold your tongue! You're disturbing the preaching; we cannot hear the silvery tones of the orator; be still. It is not proper for a beggarman like you, crawling in the street, to disturb respectable people by your harsh, grumbling voice – be quiet!" But his heart being thus moved, there was no silence for his tongue. So much the more, a great deal, with increasing vehemence and force, he iterated and reiterated the prayer, *"Jesus, Son of David, have mercy on me!" "Son of David, have mercy on me!"* Now, if you desire salvation, and have begun to pray, Satan will say, "Ah, it is of no use; be quiet!" The flesh will say, "Why this ado? There is time enough yet." Procrastination will come in and say, "When you grow old it will be time enough then to begin to seek the Lord." A thousand difficulties will be suggested, but, O soul, if you are indeed set upon salvation, and God has made you in earnest, you will say to all these, "Stand back! I cannot and will not be silenced by you. I must have mercy; it is mercy I want, and it is mercy I must have, or I perish forever, and that I cannot afford; therefore, I will cry all the more." I wish – but ah! it is not in my power – still I do wish that I could persuade you to urgent prayer.

May the Holy Spirit lead you to pray. Well do I recollect my own prayers when I was seeking Christ. I prayed even for months, and sometimes in the chamber where I sought the Lord I felt as if I could not come away from the mercy seat till I had an answer of peace, but I waited long before I got it. Still, it came at last, and oh! it is worth waiting for! If one had to plead for mercy for twenty years at a time, yet if at last the silver scepter were stretched out, it would well repay all the groanings and the tears of the most anxious spirits. Get to your chambers, then, or if you cannot get to your chambers, get to a sawpit or a hayloft; it matters not where, but pour out your heart before him, and do not rise from your knees until the Lord has said, *"[Your] sins, which are many, have been forgiven."*

After this man had thus pleaded, it is noteworthy that Jesus stood still and called him. I must call your attention to this matter. As soon as Jesus had called the blind man, the effect produced on him is startling. I think I see him sitting there by the wayside helpless. Jesus bids him to come. He gets up, and in a moment he throws off that outer garment which had been so precious to him, in which he had so often wrapped himself up on cold nights when he had to sleep beneath the open sky. That much-prized, though all-patched and filthy garment, he threw right away; it might have made him a minute or two slower, so off he threw it, and away he flung it. Ah! and it is a great mercy when a poor soul feels that it can throw away anything and everything to get to Christ. "Oh!" says the sinner who really seeks a Savior, "if there is any sin that I have indulged in that prevents my finding mercy, only let me know it, and I will put it away. Is there any habit I have which I do not even know to be sin, or a thing I do that gives me pleasure, but is objectionable in the sight of God? I will put it away. O Lord, if I must be poor, or if I must be sick, I will put away my health, and put away my wealth, if I may but find mercy.

> **You must have salvation. You cannot afford to do without it.**

> The dearest idol I have known,
>   Whate'er that idol be;
> Help me to tear it from its throne,
>   And worship only thee.

I charge you, seekers of Jesus, let nothing stand between you and Christ. You must have salvation, man. You cannot afford to do without it. O fling away, then, everything that might impede you. Cast off the garment that might trip you up in the heavenly race. Lay aside every weight, and the sin that does most easily trouble you, and press to Jesus at once. Today, I pray you, press to Jesus, with vehement speed, and be not content till you get the blessing!

Once more. When this man had come to Jesus, and Jesus said to him, *"What do you want Me to do for you?"* the man returned a straightforward and intelligent answer. He said, *"Lord, I want to regain my sight!"* Now, when you are in prayer today, any of you, do not merely pray a general prayer, but put it before the Lord in the plainest language. I could suppose, for example, the tendency of your confession and petition might be something like this – "Lord, here I am; I have lived all this time without regard to you. I have been a hearer at the tabernacle; sometimes I have been so deeply impressed that I have shed many tears. But Lord, it has all come to nothing; sermons upon sermons have I heard, yet sermon after sermon has been lost upon me. I am afraid I am a gospel-hardened sinner. I think, Lord, that sitting as I do right opposite the preacher, he speaking so pointedly as he does to me, witnessing, as I do, how others have been saved while I have been left unsaved, my heart must be like the lower millstone; yet, Lord, you can save. O have mercy on me yet! O melt this heart of stone; break this stone; thaw this rock of ice!

Lord, I know what it is that hinders me: there is that cherished sin; there is that vile companion; there is that lust of the flesh. O God, enable me to give it up! Now help me to pluck off the right arm, and tear out the right eye, for oh! I cannot perish, I cannot perish. I cannot bear your wrath in the world to come; I am afraid because of it; therefore would I flee from it, and find refuge in Jesus!" Or perhaps your case may be quite a different one, and in pleading with God you may have to say, "Lord, I never was a keeper of your Sabbath; I have been on all those holy days spending the time in sinful pleasure, and I do not know that I have any regard for you, but I fell into the crowd at the tabernacle gates just now, and got into the aisle, and Lord, your Word has found me out, and I feel as I never felt before; I do desire to be reconciled to you."

Oh! you do not know how glad your heavenly Father will be to hear that, for, just as in the parable, the father ran and fell upon the prodigal's neck and kissed him, so will our Father who is in heaven run and fall upon your guilty neck, and give you the kiss of pardon and of acceptance, and you, even you, shall be saved. Glory be to God, there is none that press, and seek, and knock, and strive thus, but that mercy shall come unto them.

Still, I cannot withhold one other remark. That which really brought salvation to this blind man was his faith, for Christ says, *"Your faith has made you well."* Now, here is the greatest point of all – faith! Faith;

for work without faith is of little worth. Faith is the great saving grace; it is the real life-germ. "What is faith?" you say. Anxious inquirer, if you would know what faith is, understand that the other word for it is *trust* – belief. The faith that saves is a belief that Jesus Christ, the Son of God, offered an atonement for sin, and then after a firm conviction, it is a simple trusting in that atonement for your salvation. Can you this night – oh! I pray the Holy Spirit enable you! – can you this night trust Jesus Christ? When I ask that question of an awakened sinner, it seems to me as if the answer should always be "Can I trust him?

Alas, indeed! Such a Savior, so divine, offering such a sacrifice as the death of his own self, surely I can trust him!" Here is a nail upon which you may well hang all the weight of the vessel. Here is a bridge over which tens of thousands of the weightiest sinners may cross safely. Come then, sinner, what say you? Are you resolved to trust Jesus? If so, your faith has saved you already; go and wrestle in prayer till you get an assurance of it.

Time flies, and I must not delay; therefore, let me have a solemn word upon another point. When Jesus was passing by, it was, as we have said, to the blind man an hour of hope, and it was an hour for rousing himself to action. Now we notice, thirdly, it was an hour of crisis.

Did I not observe just now that while life lasts Jesus is passing by? That is true in one sense, but I also believe that in many cases the hour in which they will ever be able to find mercy is past long before men die. There was a man who had listened to an earnest gospel exhortation, and as he listened he felt that the preacher was speaking out his inmost heart to him. He thought within himself, "That is an important matter." As he listened, the importance of the matter seemed to strike him more and more. His tears began to flow, and he resolved that when he reached his home that night he would seek the Lord. As he went on his way, a companion met him and said, "Come with me," and he invited him to a certain alehouse. He was revolted at the thought for the moment. He stood still, and the deliberation seemed to go on in his soul. "Which shall it be? Shall it be my jovial companion, or shall it be that earnest

> A Savior, so divine, offering the death of his own self. Here is a bridge over which tens of thousands of the weightiest sinners may cross safely.

prayer on which I have resolved?" He hesitated a moment, and his better self, or rather the Holy Spirit within him, conquered, and that night as he knelt, divine light shone into his soul, and he became a Christian.

On that same occasion there was another man who passed through precisely the same experience, and to whom the same temptation came, but he yielded to it, and he was never after that troubled with such another difficulty. He listened again to sermons, but he never felt under them as he did under that. They lost all interest in him. After a time, he left off heeding the means of grace, and he is at this time a blasphemer, though before he seemed to stand upon the very borders of salvation. Probably to this last man there will never come a day of grace again. He has now put himself beyond the reach of it as to the means; for he attends no place of worship, and gives no heed to anything of the kind. Religion has become a thing for him to laugh at, and its preachers the objects of his scorn.

Here were the turning points of these two lives: grace decided the one, and the flesh decided the other. The one, in all human probability, is bound for heaven, and the other, alas! is bound for hell. Such a night as this may have come now. I do not know that young man, nor where he sits today, but he is here. He has, after this service is over, an engagement of a sort that if his sainted mother in the country could but know of it, it would make her very hair stand on end with horror, to think that her son should have come to *that*. I charge him by the living God to give up that sin, or else this night he may seal his own damnation. There sits here in this house a woman who will this evening, if the Lord shall make her fulfill the purpose of her heart, seek Christ and find him, but if the temptation that is now striving with her should overcome her, and the evening should be spent, after all, in idle chat, then her conscience shall be seared as with a hot iron, and from this hour it shall not be possible for the shafts of the gospel to come at her. O that God may decide your case rightly for you, helping your will, your stubborn and wicked will, to yield and bow to the blessed instigation of his Holy Spirit in your hearts, for I am persuaded that this is an hour of crisis to many here.

Lastly, remember that this hour of Jesus passing by is an hour that will soon be gone.

Did you notice that word: *Jesus of Nazareth was passing by*? He is not stopping, he is passing by; for he is going on towards the walls of Jericho to pass through its gates. Blind man! it is now or never, for he is passing by. He has come up to where you are; cry to him now! He has passed you, but cry to him. Now, man, he is long past, but he can yet hear you; cry to him now! Ah! but he has passed and is gone, and the man has not cried, and now there is no other who can open his eyes, and neither will this Son of David, for he has passed by and been unasked, unsought to bless. You had Christ passing by when you were young. I wish to God you had said to him then, "Have mercy on me!" but you waited till he came up to you in middle life, and yet you did not seek him.

Alas, for that! And now the gray hairs are stealing over you, and a half-century of unbelief has hardened your heart. You are getting near to sixty years of ungodliness, but he is not out of earshot yet. He will hear you now. O cry to him, I pray you, cry; and may God's Holy Spirit, who is the author of all true begging, breathe in you now a cry that never shall be stopped until you get the answer, *"Your faith has saved you; go in peace."*

Now, it may be that some here to whom I am speaking think that this preaching is all child's play, and that our talking about these solemn things is very easy. I protest before God this night that I feel it to be stern, hard work. Not but what it is easy and delightful to preach the gospel, but I yearn over the souls of some of you. I cannot understand why you crowd here, and when I know that there are perhaps half as many outside as inside, clamoring for entrance, I know not why it is. I do nothing to attract you here, but I speak right out my Master's gospel. The truth is, if the Lord inclines your hearts and brings you within the sound of the gospel which I am eager to proclaim, I feel a responsibility for you which it is not possible for you to estimate. What if you should in the day of judgment be able to say, "We crowded to that house, and we listened to that man, but he did not tell us the truth, or he told it to us so coldly that we thought it did not matter, and we put it off!" Oh! if you are lost, still bear me witness that I would willingly have you saved, and if persuasions could bring you to Christ, you should not perish for lack of them. *"Believe in the Lord Jesus, and you will be saved."* This is the message. But, if you reject it, a weight falls on my spirit – it seems to crush me like a millstone now – the thought that you would be lost! For what is it to be lost? It is to be cast away from the presence of God, to be cast into hell, to have to suffer, and suffer forever, all that the justice of God can demand, all that the omnipotence of God can inflict.

Why, sirs, if I have but a headache, or a toothache for one brief hour, my patience can scarcely endure the torture; what must it be like to suffer such pains for a century? Man, I cannot guess what it must be like! What must it be like to have ten thousand times worse pains than these forever and ever? Why, to be dejected in mind, to be despairing, to be downcast – how bewildered it makes men! They take the knife or the poison in a fit of insanity; it may be they cannot bear their lives because of their anguish and desperation. But all the pangs, and anguish, and abandonment from which men suffer here are nothing to be compared with the woes and mental anguish of the world to come. Oh, the agony of a spirit doomed, forlorn, and accursed, upon which God shall put his foot in awful wrath and lift it up no more forever!

And there, as you lie, tormented to the heart, you will have this to be your miserable portion – I heard the gospel, but I would not heed it; Christ was put before me, but I would not acknowledge him; I was entreated to believe in his name and fly to him for salvation, but I hesitated, hung in suspense, objected, and at length denied him. And all for what? For a little drink, a little dance, a little sin that yielded me but slight pleasure, or for worldly gain, or for low and groveling vices, or for sheer carelessness and gaiety! Lost, lost, lost! and for nothing! A sinner damned! He lost his soul, but he did not gain the world. He gained only a little frivolous pleasure, even that poor chump change he spent in an hour, and then he was forever cast away! May it not be so with you – not with one of you, old or young, but the Lord have mercy upon the whole assembly, for his dear name's sake. Amen.

THE SOUL'S CRISIS

There is a time, we know not when,
    A point we know not where,
That marks the destiny of men,
    To glory or despair.

There is a line, by us unseen,
    That crosses every path;
The hidden boundary between
    God's patience and his wrath.

To pass that limit is to die,
    To die, as if by stealth:
It does not quench the beaming eye,
    Or pale the glow of health.

The conscience may be still at ease,
    The spirits light and gay;
That which is pleasing still may please,
    And care be thrust away.

But on that forehead God has set
    Indelibly a mark,
Unseen by man – for man as yet
    Is blind and in the dark.

And yet the doomed man's path below,
    Like Eden, may have bloomed;
He did not, does not, will not know,
    Or feel that he is doomed.

He knows, he feels, that all is well,
    And every fear is calm'd
He lives, he dies, he wakes in hell,
    Not only doomed but damned.

O where is thy mysterious bourne,
    By which our path is crossed,
Beyond which God himself hath sworn,
    That he who goes is lost?

How far may we go on in sin?
    How long will God forbear?
Where does hope end? and where begin
    The confines of despair?

An answer from the skies is sent –
    "Ye that from God depart,
While it is called today, Repent!
    And harden not your heart."

Chapter 6

Saving Faith

"Your faith has saved you." (Luke 7:50)

"Your faith has made you well." (Luke 18:42)

I do not remember if this expression is found anywhere else in the Word of God. It is found in these two places in the Gospel of Luke, but not in any other Gospel. Luke also gives us in two other places a kindred and an almost identical expression: *"Your faith has made you well."* This you will find used in reference to the woman whose issue of blood had been extinguished (Luke 8:48), and in connection with that one of the ten lepers who returned to praise the Savior for the cure he had received (Luke 17:19). You will find the expression, *"Your faith has made you well,"* once in Matthew and twice in Mark, but you find it twice in Luke, and together with that the words of our text, *"Your faith has saved you."* Are we wrong in supposing that the long intercourse of Luke with the apostle Paul led him not only to receive the great doctrine of justification by faith which Paul so plainly taught, and to attach to faith that high importance which Paul always did, but also to have a peculiar memory for those expressions which were used by the Savior, in which faith was decidedly honored to a very high degree?

Albeit Luke would not have written anything which was not true for the sake of maintaining the grand doctrine so clearly taught by the apostle, yet I think his full conviction of it would help to recall to his memory more vividly those words of the Lord Jesus from which it could be more clearly learned or illustrated. Be that as it may, we know that Luke was inspired, and that he has written neither more nor less than what the Savior actually said, and therefore we may be quite sure that the expression, *"Your faith has saved you,"* fell from the Redeemer's lips, and we are bound to accept it as pure unquestionable truth, and we may repeat it ourselves without fear of misleading others, or encroaching upon any other truth.

I mention this because the other day I heard an earnest friend say that faith did not save us, at which announcement I was rather surprised. The brother, it is true, qualified the expression, and showed that he meant to make it clear that Jesus saved us, and not our own act of faith. I agreed with what he meant, but not with what he said, for he had no right to use an expression which was in flat contradiction to the distinct declaration of the Savior: *"Your faith has saved you."* We are not to strain any expression to make it mean more than the speaker intended, and it is well to guard words from being misunderstood; but on the other hand, we may not quite go so far as to absolutely negate a declaration of the Lord himself, however we may mean to qualify it. It is to be qualified if you like, but it is not to be contradicted, for there it stands: *"Your faith has saved you."* Now we shall, by God's help, inquire, What was it that saved the two persons whose history will come before us? It was their faith. Our second inquiry will be, What kind of faith was it that saved them? And then thirdly, What does this teach us in reference to faith?

What was it that saved the two persons whose history we are about to consider?

In the repentant woman's case, her great sins were forgiven her and she became a woman of extraordinary love; she loved much, for she had been forgiven much. I feel, in thinking of her, something like an eminent father of the church who said, "This narrative is not one which I can well preach upon; I had far rather weep over it in secret." That woman's tears, that woman's unbraided tresses wiping the Savior's feet, her coming so near to her Lord in such company, facing such proud nitpickers with such fond and resolute intent of doing honor to Jesus, truly, among those that have loved the Savior, there has not lived a greater one than this woman who was a sinner. Yet for all that, Jesus did not say to her, "Your love has saved you." Love is a golden apple of the tree of which faith is the root, and the Savior took care not to ascribe to the fruit that which belongs only to the root. This loving woman was also very notable for her repentance.

Mark you well those tears. Those were no tears of sentimental emotion, but a rain of holy heart-sorrow for sin. She had been a sinner and she knew it; she remembered well her multitude of iniquities, and she felt each sin deserved a tear, and there she stood weeping herself away because she had offended her dear Lord. Yet it is not said, "Your repentance has saved you." Her being saved caused her repentance, but repentance did not save her. Sorrow for sin is an early token of grace within the heart, yet it is nowhere said, "Your sorrow for sin has saved you." She was a woman of great humility. She came behind the Lord and washed his feet, as though she felt herself only able to be a menial servant to perform works of drudgery, and to find a pleasure in so serving her Lord. Her reverence for him had reached a very high point; she regarded him as a king, and she did what has sometimes been done for monarchs by zealous subjects – she kissed the feet of her heart's Lord, who well deserved the homage. Her loyal reverence led her to kiss the feet of her Lord, the sovereign of her soul, but I do not find that Jesus said, "Your humility has saved you," or that he said, "Your reverence has saved you." But he put the crown upon the head of her faith and said explicitly, *"Your faith has made you well; go in peace."*

In the case of the blind man to whom my second text refers – this man was notable for his earnestness; he cried, and cried aloud, *"Son of David, have mercy on me!"* He was notable for his compulsion, for they who would have silenced him rebuked him in vain; he cried so much the more, *"Son of David, have mercy on me!"* But I do not discover that Christ attributed his salvation to his prayers, earnest and compelling though they were. It is not written, "Your prayers have saved you"; it is written, *"Your faith has made you well."* He was a man of considerable and clear knowledge, and he had a distinct understanding of the true character of Christ. He scorned to call him *Jesus of Nazareth,* as the crowd did, but he proclaimed him *"Son of David,"* and in the presence of that throng he dared profess his full conviction that the humble man, dressed in a peasant's garb, who was threading his way through the throng, was none other than the royal heir of the royal line of Judah, and was indeed the fulfiller of the type of David, the expected Messiah, the King of the Jews, the Son of David. Yet I do not find that Jesus attributed his salvation to his knowledge, to his clear understanding, or to his distinct assertion of his messiahship; but he said to him, *"Your faith has made you well,"* laying the entire stress of his salvation upon his faith.

This being so in both cases, we are led to ask, What is the reason for it? What is the reason why in every case, in every man that is saved, faith is the great instrument of salvation? Is it not first because God has a right to choose what way of salvation he pleases, and he has chosen that men should be saved not by their works, but by their faith in his dear Son? God has a right to give his mercy to whom he pleases; he has a right to give it when he pleases; he has a right to give it in what mode he pleases. And know this, O sons of men, that the decree of heaven is immutable, and stands fast forever – *"He who has believed and has been baptized shall be saved; but he who has disbelieved shall be condemned."*

To this there shall be no exception; the Lord has made the rule and it shall stand. If you want to have salvation, *"believe in the Lord Jesus, and you will be saved";* but if not, salvation is utterly impossible to you. This is the appointed way; follow it, and it leads to heaven; refuse it, and you must perish. This is God's sovereign determination: *"He who believes in Him is not judged; he who does not believe has been judged already, because he has not believed in the name of the only begotten Son of God."* The Lord's will be done. If this be his method of grace, let us not kick against it. If he determines that faith shall save, so let it be; only, Good Master, create and increase our faith.

But while I attribute this to the sovereign choice of God, I do see, for Scripture plainly indicates it, a reason in the nature of things why faith should thus have been selected. The apostle tells us it is of faith that it might be of grace. If the condition of salvation had been either feeling or working, then, such is the depravity of our nature, that we would inevitably have attributed the merit of salvation to the working or the feeling. We would have claimed something by which to glory. It matters not how low the condition may have been, man would have still considered that there was something required of him, that something came from him, and that, therefore, he might take some credit to himself. But no man, unless he be demented, ever claims credit for believing the truth. If he hears that which convinces him, he is convinced; and if he is persuaded, he is persuaded; but he feels that it could not well be otherwise. He attributes the effect to the truth and the influence used. He does not go about and boast because he believes what is so clear to him that he cannot doubt it. If he did so boast of spiritual faith, all thinking men would say at once, "Why do you boast in the fact of having believed, and especially when this believing would never have been yours if it had not been for the force of the truth which convinced you, and the working of the Spirit of God which constrained you to believe?"

Faith is chosen by Christ to wear the crown of salvation because – let me contradict myself – it refuses to wear the crown. It was Christ who saved the repentant woman; it was Christ who saved that blind beggar, but he takes the crown from off his own head, so dear is faith to him, and he puts the diadem upon the head of faith and says, *"Your faith has saved you,"* because he is absolutely certain that faith will never take the glory to herself, but will again lay the crown at the pierced feet, and say, "Not unto myself be glory, for you have done it; you are the Savior, and you alone." In order, then, to illustrate and to protect the interests of sovereign grace, and to shut out all vain glorying, God has been pleased to make the way of salvation to be by faith, and by no other means.

Nor is this all. It is clear to everyone who chooses to think that in the order of the renewal of the heart, which is the chief part of salvation, it is well to begin with faith, because faith once rightly exercised becomes the mainspring of the entire nature. The man believes that he is forgiven. What then? He feels gratitude to him who has pardoned him. Feeling gratitude, it is but natural that he should hate that which displeases his Savior, and should love intensely that which is pleasing to him who saved him, so that faith operates upon the entire nature, and becomes the instrument in the hand of the regenerating Spirit by which all the faculties of the soul are put into the right condition.

As a man thinks in his heart so is he, but his thinking comes out of his beliefs; if he be put right in his beliefs, then his understanding will operate upon his affections, and all the other powers of his manhood, and old things will pass away, and all things will become new through the wonderful effect of the faith, which is of the operation of God. Faith works by love, and through love it purifies the soul, and the man becomes a new creature. Do you see, then, the wisdom of God? He may choose what way he will, but he chooses a way which at once guards his grace from our felonious boastings, and on the other hand produces in us a holiness which otherwise never would have been there.

Faith in salvation, however, is not the meritorious cause, nor is it in any sense the salvation itself. Faith saves us just as the mouth saves from hunger. If we are hungry, bread is the real cure for hunger, but still it would be right to say that eating removes hunger, seeing that the bread itself could not benefit us unless the mouth eats it. Faith is the soul's mouth whereby the hunger of the heart is removed. Christ also is the brazen serpent lifted up; all the healing virtue is in him, and yet no healing virtue comes out of the brazen serpent to any who will not look, so that the looking is rightly considered to be the act which saves. True, in the deepest sense it is Christ uplifted who saves, to him be all the glory; but without looking to him you cannot be saved, so that "there is life in a look," as well as life in the Savior to whom you look. Nothing is yours until you appropriate it. If you are enriched, the thing appropriated enriches you; yet it is not incorrect but strictly right to say it is the appropriation of the blessing which makes you rich. Faith is the hand of the soul. Stretched out, it lays hold of the salvation of Christ, and so by faith we are saved. *"Your faith has made you well."* I need not dwell longer on that point. It is self-evident from the text that faith is the great means of salvation.

What kind of faith was it that saved these people? I will mention, first, the essential *agreements,* and then, secondly, the *differentia,* or the points in which this faith differed in its external manifestations in the two cases.

In the instances of the repentant woman and the blind beggar, their faith was fixed alone in Jesus. You cannot discover anything floating in their faith in Jesus which adulterated it; it was unmixed faith in him. The woman pressed forward to *him;* her tears fell on *him;* her ointment was for *him;* her unloosed tresses were a towel for *his* feet; she cared for no one else, not even for the disciples whom she respected for his sake; her whole spirit and soul were absorbed in *him.* He could save her, he could blot out her sins. She believed him, she did it unto him. The same was the case with that blind man. He had no thought of any ceremonies to be performed by priests; he had no idea of any medicine which might be given him by physicians. His cry was, *"Son of David," "Son of David."* The only notice he took of others was to disregard them, and still to cry, *"Son of David," "Son of David." "What do you want **Me** to do for you?"* (emphasis added) was the Lord's question, and it answered to the desire of his soul, for he knew that if anything were done, it must be done by the Son of David. It is essential that our faith must rest alone on Jesus. Mix anything with Christ, and you are undone. If your faith shall stand with one foot upon the rock of his merits, and the other foot upon the sand of your own duties, it will fall, and great will be the fall thereof. Build wholly on the rock, for if so much as a corner of the edifice shall rest on anything besides, it will ensure the ruin of the whole.

> None but Jesus, none but Jesus
> Can do helpless sinners good.

All true faith is alike in this respect.

The faith of these two was alike in its confession of unworthiness. What was meant by her standing behind? What was meant by her tears, her ever-flowing tears, but that she felt unworthy to draw near to Jesus? And what was meant by the beggar's cry, *"Have mercy on me"*? Note the stress he lays upon it. *"Have **mercy** on me"* (emphasis added). He does not claim the cure by merit, nor ask it as a reward. To mercy he appealed. Now I care not whose faith it is, whether it be that of David in his bitter cries of the fifty-first psalm, or whether it be that of Paul in his highest exaltation upon being without condemnation through Christ. There is always in connection with true faith a thorough and deep sense that it is mercy, and mercy alone, which saves us from the wrath to come. Dear hearer, do not deceive yourself. Faith and boasting are as opposite to one another as the two poles. If you come before Christ with your righteousness in your hand, you come without faith; but if you come with faith you must also come with confession of sin, for true faith always walks hand in hand with a deep sense of guiltiness before the Most High. This is so in every case.

Their faith was alike, moreover, in defying and conquering opposition. Little do we know the inward struggles of the repentant woman as she crossed the threshold of Simon's house. "He will repel you," the stern, cold Pharisee will say. "Get you gone, you whore; how dare you defile the doors of honest men." But whatever may happen she passes through the door; she comes to where the feet of the Savior are stretched out towards the entrance as he is reclining at the table, and there she stands. Simon glanced at her. He thought the glance would wither her, but her love for Christ was too well rooted to be withered by him. No doubt he made many signs of his displeasure, and showed that he was horrified at such a creature being anywhere near him, but she took no notice of him. Her Lord was there, and she felt safe. Timid as a dove, she trembled not while he was near, and she returned no defiant glances for Simon's haughty looks; her eyes were occupied with weeping. She did not turn aside to demand an explanation for his unkind motions, for her lips were all engrossed with kissing those dear feet. Her Lord, her Lord, was all to her. She overcame through faith in him, and held her ground, and did not leave the house till he dismissed her with *"Go in peace."*

It was the same with the blind man. He said, *"Son of David, have mercy on me!"* They cried, "Hush! Why these outcries, blind beggar? His eloquence is music; do not interrupt him. Never a man spoke as he is speaking. Every tone rings like the harps of the angels. Hush! How dare you spoil his discourse?" But over and above them all went up the urgent prayer, *"Son of David, have mercy on me!"* and he prevailed. All true faith is opposed. If your faith is never tested, it is not born of the race of the church militant. *This is the victory that has overcome the world—our faith,* but it is indicated in that very declaration that there must be something to overcome, and that faith must wage war for its existence.

Once more, the faith of these two persons was alike in being openly declared. I will not say that the declaration took the same form in both, for it did not; but still it was equally open. There is the Savior, and there comes the weeping, repentant woman. She loves him. Is she ashamed to say so? It may bring her reproach; it will certainly rake up the old reproaches against her, for she has been a sinner. But never mind what she has been, nor who may be present to see her. She loves her Lord, and she will show it. She will bring the ointment and she will anoint his feet, even in the presence of Pharisees, Pharisees who would say, "Is this one of the disciples of Christ? A pretty convert to boast of! A fine conquest this is, for his kingdom! A harlot becomes a disciple! What next and what next?" She must have known and felt all that, but still there was no concealment. She loved her Lord, and she would affirm it, and so in the very house of the Pharisee, there being no other opportunity so convenient, she comes forward, and without words, but with actions far more eloquent than words, she says, "I love him. These tears shall show it; this ointment shall diffuse the knowledge of it, as its sweet perfume fills the room; and every lock of my hair shall be a witness that I am my Lord's and he is mine." She professed her faith.

And so did the blind man. He did not sit there and say, "I know he is the Son of David, but I must not say it." They said, some of them contemptuously, and others indifferently, "It is Jesus of Nazareth." But he will not have it so. *"Jesus, Son of David,"* says he; and loud above their noise I hear him cry, like a herald proclaiming the King, *"Son of David."* Why, sirs, it seems to me he was exalted to a high office: he became the herald of the King, and proclaimed him, and this belongs to a high officer of state in our country. The blind beggar showed great decision and courage. He cried in effect, "Son of David you are; Son of David I proclaim you; Son of David you shall be proclaimed, whoever may oppose it; only turn your eyes and have mercy upon me."

Are there any of you here who have a faith in Christ which you are ashamed of? I also am ashamed of you, and so also will Christ be ashamed of you when he comes in the glory of his Father and all his holy angels with him. Ashamed to claim that you are honest? Then I think you must live in bad company, where to be a rogue is to be famous; and if you are ashamed to say, "I love my Lord," I think you are courting the friendship of Christ's enemies, and what can you be but an enemy yourself? If you love him, say it. Put on your Master's regimentals, enlist in his army, and come forward and declare, *"As for me and my house, we will serve the Lord."* Their faith was alike, then, in these four particulars: it was fixed alone on him, it was accompanied with a sense of unworthiness, it struggled and conquered opposition, and it openly declared itself before all comers.

By your patience I shall now try to show the *differences* between the same faith as to its manifestations. First, the woman's faith acted like a woman's faith. She showed tender love, and the affections are the glory and the strength of women. They were certainly such in her. Her love was intense, womanly love, and she poured it out upon the Savior. The man's faith acted like a man's in its determination and strength. He persisted in crying, *"Jesus, Son of David."* There was as much that was masculine about his faith as there was of the feminine in the repentant woman's faith, and everything should be in its order and after its season. It would not have been proper for the woman's voice to be heard so boldly above the crowd; it would have seemed out of place for a man's tears to have been falling upon the Savior's feet. Either one or the other might have been justifiable, but they would not have been equally suitable. But now they are as suitable as they are excellent.

The woman acts as a godly woman should, the man like a godly man. Never let us measure ourselves by other people. Do not, my brother, say, "I could not shed tears." Who asked you to do so? A man's tears are mostly within, and so let them be; it is ours to use other modes of showing our love. And, my sister, do not say, "I could not act as a herald and publicly proclaim the King." I doubt not you could do so if there were need, but your tears in secret, and those wordless tokens of love for Jesus which you are rendering, are not less acceptable because they are not the same as a man would give. No, they are the better because they are more suitable to you. Do not think that all the flowers of God's garden must bloom in the same color or shed the same perfume.

Notice next that the woman acted like a woman who had been a sinner. What was more fitting than tears? What fitter place for her than at the Savior's feet? She had been a sinner, she acts like a sinner; but the man who had been a beggar acted like a beggar. What does a beggar do but cry out for charity? Did he not beg gloriously? Never one plied the trade more earnestly than he. *"Son of David,"* said he, *"have mercy on me!"* I would not have liked to have seen the beggar sitting there weeping, nor to have heard the repentant woman shouting. Neither one would have been natural or seemly. Faith works according to the condition, circumstances, gender, or ability of the person in whom it lives, and it best shows itself in its own form, not in an artificial manner, but in the natural outflow of the heart.

Observe, also, that the woman did not speak. There is something very beautiful in the golden silence of the woman, which was richer than her silver speech would have been. But the man was not silent; he spoke, he spoke out, and his words were excellent. I venture to say that the woman's silence spoke as powerfully as the man's voice. Of the two I think I find more eloquence in the tears moistening, and the unbraided hair wiping the Savior's feet, than in the cry, *"Son of David, have mercy on me!"* Yet both forms of expression were equally good: the silence best in the woman with her tears, and the speech best in the man with his confident trust in Christ. Do not think it necessary, dear friend, in order to serve, that you do other people's work. What your own hand finds to do, do it with all your might. If you think you can never honor Christ till you enter a pulpit, it may be just possible that you will afterwards honor him best by getting out of it as quickly as you can. There have been persons well qualified to adorn the religion of Christ with a lapstone of a shoemaker on their lap who have thought it necessary to mount a pulpit, and in that position have been a hindrance to Christ and his gospel.

Sister, there is a sphere for you, so keep to it, and let none push you out of it; but do not think there is nothing else to do except the work which some other woman does. God has called her, let her follow God's voice; he calls you in another direction, follow his voice there. You will be most like that other excellent woman when you are most different from her. I mean that you will be most truly obedient to Christ, as she is, if you pursue quite another path.

There was a difference, again, in this. The woman gave – she brought her ointment. The man did the opposite – he begged. There are various ways of showing love for Christ which are equally excellent tokens of faith. To give him of her ointment, and give him of her tears, and give him the accommodation of her hair, was good; it showed her faith, which worked by love. To give nothing, for the beggar had nothing to give, but simply to honor Christ by appealing to his generosity and his royal power, was best in the beggar. I can commend neither above the other, for I doubt not that both the repentant woman and the beggar gave Christ their whole heart, and what more does Jesus ask for from anyone?

The thoughts of the woman and the thoughts of the beggar were different too. Her thoughts were mainly about the past and her sins – therefore her tears. To be forgiven, that was her point. His thoughts were mainly about the present, and did not so much concern his sin as his deficiency, infirmity, and inability, and so he came with different thoughts. I do not doubt that he thought of sin, as I dare say she also thought of infirmity; but in her case the thought of sin was uppermost, and therefore the tears; in his case the infirmity was uppermost, and therefore the prayer, *"Lord, I want to regain my sight!"* Do not, then, compare your experience with that of another.

God is a God of wonderful variety. The painter who repeats himself in many pictures has a deficiency of conception, but the master artist scarcely ever sketches the same thing a second time. There is a boundless variety in genius, and God, who transcends all the genius of men, creates an infinite variety in the works of his grace. Look not, therefore, for likeness everywhere. The woman, it is said, loved much, and she proved her love by her acts; but the man loved much too, and showed his love by actions which were most admirable, for he followed Jesus along the way, glorifying God. Yet they were different actions. I do not find that he brought any box of ointment, or anointed Christ's feet; neither do I find that she literally followed Christ along the way, though no doubt she followed him in the spirit; neither did she with a loud voice glorify God as the restored blind beggar did. There are differences of operation, but the same Lord; there are differences of capacity and differences of calling, and by this reflection I hope you will be enabled to deliver yourselves from the fault of judging one by another, and that you will look for the same faith, but not for the same development of it.

So interesting is this subject that I want you to follow me while I very rapidly sketch the woman's case, and then the man's, not mentioning the differences one by one, but allowing the two pictures to impress themselves separately upon your minds.

Observe this woman. What a strange compound she was. She was consciously unworthy, and therefore she wept, yet she drew very near to Jesus. Her acts were those of nearness and communion; she washed his feet with her tears, she wiped them with the hairs of her head, and meanwhile she kissed them again and again. *"She, . . . has not ceased to kiss My feet,"* said Christ. A sense of unworthiness and the enjoyment of communion were mixed together. Oh, divine faith which blends the two! She was shamefaced, yet was she very bold. She dared not look the Master in the face as yet, so she approached him from behind; yet she dared to face Simon, and remain in his room, whether he frowned or not. I have known some who have blushed in the face of Christ who would not have blushed before a judge, nor at the stake, if they had been dragged there for Christ's sake. Such a woman was Anne Askew, humble before her Master, but like a lioness before the foes of God.

The repentant woman wept, she was a mourner, yet she had a deep joy; I know she did, for every kiss meant joy. Every time she lifted that blessed foot and kissed it, her heart leaped with the exhilaration of love. Her heart knew bitterness for sin, but it knew also the sweetness of pardon. What a mixture! Faith made the compound. She was humble, never one more so; yet see how she takes upon herself to deal with the King himself.

Brethren, you and I are satisfied, and well we may be, if we may wash the saints' feet, but she was not. Oh, the courage of this woman! She will pass through the outer court, and get right to the King's own throne, and there pay her homage, in her own person, to his person, and wash the feet of the Wonderful, the Counselor, the mighty God. I know not that an angel ever performed such service, and therefore this woman takes preeminence as having done for Jesus what no other being ever did. I have said that she was silent, and yet she spoke. I will add that she was despised, but Christ set her high in honor, and made Simon, who despised her, to feel little in her presence. I will also add that she was a great sinner, but she was a great saint. Her great sinnership, when pardoned, became the raw stuff out of which great saints are made by the mighty power of God. Finally, she was saved by faith, so says the text, but if ever there was a case in which James could not have said, "Shall faith save you?" and in which he must have said, "Here is one that shows her faith by her works," it was the case of this woman. There she is before you. Imitate her faith itself, though you cannot actually copy her deeds.

Now look at the man. He was blind, but he could see a great deal more than the Pharisees who said they could see. Blind, but his inward optics saw the King in his beauty, saw the splendor of his throne, and he confessed it. He was a beggar, but he had a royal soul and a strong, sovereign determination that was not to be put down. He had the kind of mind which dwells in men who are princes among their fellows. He is not to be stopped by disciples, no, nor by apostles. He has begun to pray, and pray he will till he obtains the help he seeks.

Note well that what he knew he professed, what he desired he pleaded for, and what he needed he understood. *"Lord, I want to regain my sight!"* He was clear about his needs, and clear about the only person who could supply them. What he asked for he expected, for when he was bidden to come, he evidently expected that his sight would be restored, for we are told by another Gospel writer that he threw aside his beggar's cloak. He felt he would never want to beg again. He was sure his eyes were about to be opened. Lastly, what he received he was grateful for, for as soon as he could walk without a guide he took Christ to be his guide, and followed him along the way, glorifying him. Look on both pictures. May you have the shadows and the lights of both, as far as they would tend to make you also another and distinct picture by the selfsame artist, whose hand alone can produce such wonders.

> The women's great sinnership, when pardoned, became the raw stuff out of which great saints are made by the mighty power of God.

What does this teach us in reference to faith? It teaches us first that faith is all-important. Do, I pray you, my hearers, see whether you have the precious faith, the faith of God's elect. Remember there are not many things in Scripture called *precious,* but there is the *precious blood,* and there goes with it the *precious faith.* If you do not have that, you are lost; if you do not have that, you are neither fit to live nor fit to die; if you do not have that, your eternal destiny will be infinite despair. But if you have faith, though it be as a grain of mustard seed, you are saved. *"Your faith has made you well."*

Learn next that the main matter in faith is the person whom you believe. I do not say *in* whom you believe. That would be true, but not quite so scriptural an expression. Paul does not say, as I hear most people quote it, "I know *in* whom I have believed." Faith believes Christ. Your faith must recognize him as a person, and come to him as a person, and rest not in his teaching merely, or his work only, but in him. *"Come to **Me**, all who are weary and heavy-laden, and **I** will give you rest"* (emphasis added). A personal Savior for sinners! Are you resting on him alone? Do you believe him? You know the safety of the building depends mainly upon the foundation, and if the foundation is not right, you may build as you will, but it will not last. Do you build, then, on Christ alone? Inquire about that as a special point.

Observe, next, that we must not expect exactly the same manifestation in each convert. Let not the elders of the church expect it; let not parents require it from their children; let not anxious friends look for it; do not expect it in yourself. Biographies are very useful, but they may become a snare. I must not judge that I am not a child of God because I am not precisely like that good man whose life I have just been reading about. Am I resting in Christ? Do I believe him? Then it may be the Lord's grace is striking out quite a different path for me from that which has been trodden by my brother, that it may illustrate other phases of its power, and show to principalities and powers the exceeding riches of divine love.

And, lastly, the matter which sums up all is this: if we have faith in Jesus we are saved, and we ought not to talk or act as if there were any question about it. *"Your faith has made you well."* Jesus says it. Granted, you have faith in Christ, and it is certain that faith has saved you. Do not, therefore, go on talking and acting and feeling as if you were not saved. I know a company of saved people who say every Sabbath, "Lord, have mercy upon us, miserable sinners"; but they are not miserable sinners if they are saved, and for them to use such words is to throw an insult upon the salvation which Christ has given them. If they are saved sinners, they ought to be rejoicing saints. What some say, others do not say, but they act as if it were so. They go about asking God to give them the mercy they have already obtained, hoping one day to receive what Christ assures them is already in their possession, talking to others as if it were a matter of question whether they were saved or not, when it cannot be a matter of question. *"Your faith has made you well."* Imagine the poor repentant woman turning around and saying to the Savior, "Lord, I humbly hope that it is true." There would have been neither humility nor faith in such an expression. Imagine that blind man, when Christ said, *"Your faith has made you well,"* saying, "I trust that in future years it will be found to be so." It would be a contradiction at once of his own earnest character and of Christ's honesty of speech. If you have believed, you are saved. Do not talk as if you were not, but now down from the willows take your harp, and sing unto the Lord a new song.

I have noticed in many prayers a tendency to avoid speaking as if facts were facts. I have heard this kind of expression: "The Lord has done great things for us by which *we desire* to be glad." The text in Psalms is, *The Lord has done great things for us; we are glad;* and if the Lord has done these great things for us, our right is to be glad about them, not to go with an infamous "if" upon our lips before the Lord who cannot lie. If you are dealing with your fellow creatures, suspect them, for they mostly deserve it; if you are listening to their promises, doubt them, for their promises go to be broken. But if you are dealing with your Lord and Master, never suspect him, for he is beyond suspicion; never doubt his promises, for heaven and earth and hell shall pass away, but not one letter or stroke of his Word shall fail. I claim for Christ that you cast away forever all the talk which is made up of "buts," and "ifs," and "perhapses," and "I hope," and "I trust." You are in the presence of One who said, *"Truly, truly,"* and meant what he said, who is *"the Amen, the faithful and true Witness."*

You would not spit in his face if he were here, yet your "ifs" and "buts" are so much insult cast upon his truth. You would not scourge him, but what do your doubts do but vex him and put him to shame?

> If you are dealing with your Lord, never doubt his promises, for heaven and earth shall pass away, but not one letter of his Word shall fail.

If he lies, never believe him; if he speaks the truth, never doubt him. Then shall you know when you have cast aside your wicked unbelief, that your faith has saved you, and you will go in peace.

Chapter 7

Compassion for the Multitude

They said to Him, "We have here only five loaves and two fish." And He said, "Bring them here to Me."
(Matthew 14:17-18)

As was Christ, my brethren, when in this world, so are we also. Such indeed is our calling of God. As Jesus was *the true Light which, coming into the world, enlightens every man,* so he said to his disciples, *"You are the light of the world."* How memorable are those words of our Lord – *"As You sent Me into the world, I also have sent them into the world."* And how weighty are those expressions of the apostle – *We beg you on behalf of Christ* – *And working together with Him.* There is something more than an interesting parallel that I want you to observe. A rich allegory appears to be couched in the simple record of the Gospel writers. The history of Christ is in type a history of his church. A skillful reader would soon think this matter out. You will remember how Christ's church was wrapped in swaddling cloths at the first, how she was laid in the manger of obscurity, how her life was conspired against by heathen kings. You will remember her baptism of the Holy Spirit, her trials and her temptations in the wilderness. The life of Christ afterwards will soon be thought out by you as shadowing forth a picture of the career of the church.

There is scarcely any point in the entire history of Jesus, from the manger at Bethlehem to the garden of Gethsemane, which is not besides its personal narrative, also a typical and pictorial history of his church. Thus the Lord has been pleased to bequeath to his church a great example written in his own holy life. As he raised the dead, so is she to do it through his Spirit that dwells in her. As he healed the sick, so is she to carry on a great healing ministry throughout the world. Or to come to our text, as Christ fed the hungry, so the church wherever she meets with those who hunger and thirst after righteousness is to bless them in the name of him who has said, *"They shall be satisfied."* Your business as a church today, and my business as a member of the church of Christ, is to feed hungry souls who are perishing for lack of knowledge with the Bread of Life. The case before us we think will furnish a noble picture of our duty, of our mission, and of what we expect the Master to do for us that we may work mightily for him.

Let us endeavor first to glance at the whole scene, collecting into harmony the accounts given by the four Gospel writers; and afterwards we shall proceed to consider two practical lessons to be deduced from it.

This miracle is recorded by Matthew, Mark, Luke, and John. There is some little divergence in each, as there naturally would be, for no four spectators could give the same description of any one scene. But what one omits, another supplies; a point that will be most interesting to one, has failed to strike another, while a third has been interested in something which the fourth has altogether omitted. It appears that Christ had sought out a waste region near to the town of Bethsaida. Bethsaida was a place which he had frequently visited. Earnestly, on another occasion, did he warn Bethsaida and Chorazin, reminding them that their privileges would rise up in judgment against them to condemn them for their unbelief. He had sought out this waste place for the purpose of retreat, for the sake of both himself and his disciples, that they might rest from their weary toils.

The people follow him; they swarm him all day long. He preaches to them the gospel; he heals their sick; and it was somewhere in the afternoon that the Master, ever patient and having divine foreknowledge of human needs, calls Philip to himself. Now, Philip was of Bethsaida, and he said to Philip, *"Where are we to buy bread, so that these may eat?"* This he said to test him to see whether his faith was proof against misgiving. Had Philip been a wise disciple he would have replied, "Master, you can feed them." But he was a weak follower of the mighty Lord. You know he afterwards proved his ignorance by saying, *"Lord, show us the Father, and it is enough for us";* and he then received a mild rebuke – *"Have I been so long with you, and yet you have not come to know Me?"* On this, Philip shows that he has not yet learned the lesson of faith. He cannot believe in anything he cannot see with the eyes of sense. Puzzled and amazed, he commits himself to his fellow disciples to talk over the matter.

Now, Andrew suggests that there is a lad nearby who has five barley loaves and a few small fish. Certainly Andrew thinks that though they will not be enough, *it is their duty to do their best.* So the loaves and fish are purchased out of the scanty store that Judas handed out, not perhaps without some grief to his heart that he should have to look so much after other people. As the day wears on, and the sun begins to set, the disciples come to the Master. Though the proposal had been suggested by him, they seem to think he has forgotten it. So they come to him and say, "Master, send the multitude away." They had thought over the problem of how to feed these people, and had come to the conclusion that they could not do it. Since they could not feed them, the next best thing would be to send them away to provide for themselves. Since they could not supply their necessities, they would endeavor to shut their eyes to their needs. "Master, send them away; let them go and buy for themselves." The Master promptly replies, *"They do not need to go away,"* there is no necessity for it; *"you give them something to eat!"* Indeed, he spoke wisely. Why should hungry men depart from the householder, from him who feeds all things, who opens his hand and satisfies the desire of every living thing?

"You give them something to eat!" said he, so that he might bring out from them a fair acknowledgment of their poverty. "Master," they said, "we have here but five barley loaves and a few small fish, *but what are these for so many people?"* Lifting up their eyes upon the vast assembled mass, they roughly calculate that there must be five thousand men, beside

a fair complement of women and of children. The Master bids them to bring those loaves and fish. He takes them, but before he breaks them, being a God of order, he bids the people to sit down in groups. Mark, who is always such a keen observer, and paints, like Hogarth, all the little minutiae of the picture – says they sat down on the green grass, as if it were exceedingly abundant and lush right there. Then he adds, they sat down by groups, afterwards using a word which is translated "in ranks" in our version, but the Greek is such as you would use if you spoke of a long range of beds in a flower garden – *parterres.* They sat down in green beds, as it were, with walks in between them. Mark seems to have gotten the idea that they were like a number of flowers whom his Master went around to water.

When they had all thus sat down, so that the strong might not struggle for the bread and tread it underfoot, and that the weak might not be neglected, all were placed in their rows, and then the Master lifted up his eyes before them all, asked a blessing, broke the bread, and gave it to the disciples, along with the fish. The disciples went around and distributed to each man, to each woman, and to each child, and they ate. They had been fasting all day long, so I dare say we should not be very far wrong if, following the example of a countryman whom I once heard, we laid a marked emphasis on the word *ate* – *They all ate.* They ate till their hunger was appeased; they ate till they were filled; they ate till they were abundantly satisfied. Then, I could suppose, on the table, or on a spot of the green grass where Christ had laid out the first bread and fish, the fragments that lay there had in the meantime multiplied. One does not like the idea of the disciples going around to gather up the odds and ends and crumbs that had fallen from each man; one would hardly think it would have been proper. But here was bread that was not injured, that had not fallen in the dust or the mire – fragments, and they gathered up more than they had at first. Here too we have a wonder. Things had been multiplied by division, and had been added to by subtraction. More was left than there had been at the start. No doubt that was done to disarm doubt and to defeat skepticism.

In later days, some of those men might say, "True, we did eat and were satisfied, or it seemed as if we did, but it might have been in a kind of dream." That bread which was left, the twelve full baskets, furnished something solid for them to look at, so that they might not think it an illusion. They gathered up the twelve full baskets. This seems to be the crowning part of the miracle. Our Lord himself, in referring to the miracle in later days, constantly says, "When we fed five thousand with five barley loaves, how many baskets did you have? And when we fed four thousand, how many full baskets did you take up?" as if the taking up of the full baskets at the end was the clenching of the nail to drive home the blessed argument that Jesus is the Christ, the Son of God, who gave his people bread to eat, even as Moses fed the Israelites with manna in the wilderness.

Having thus considered the facts, we shall take them as a basis upon which to build, God helping us, two practical lessons. The text and the miracle itself teach us, first, *our mission and our weakness,* and secondly, *our line of duty and Christ's strength.*

We are clearly taught here our mission and our weakness. Our mission! Behold before you, disciples of Christ, this very day, thousands of men, and women, and children who are hungering for the Bread of Life. They hunger till they faint. They spend their money for that which is not bread, and their labor for that which does not satisfy. They fall down famished in your highways, perishing for lack of knowledge. Still worse, when they faint, there are some who pretend to feed them. Superstition goes about, and offers them stones instead of bread, and serpents instead of fish. The Roman Catholic and the ceremonialist offer to sell these hungry souls something to gratify them. They try to feed them, but it will not satisfy; they do but eat the wind and swallow the whirlwind. The infidel tries to persuade them that they are not hungry, they are only a little nervous; thus he mocks their appetite. As soon will the body be satisfied with bubbles, or the mouth be filled with shadows, as the soul be satisfied with delusions and inventions of man. They faint; they famish; they are ready to die. Those who pretend to supply them do but mock and tantalize their needs. Nor can they feed themselves; their wallets are empty.

When Adam fell, he reduced to poverty all his posterity; neither man, nor woman, nor child among them is able to satisfy his or her own hunger. The ten thousands of your race in this land – in Europe, in Asia, in Africa, in America, and Australia – not one among them, should they all subscribe together, could find so much as one loaf upon which a single soul might feed. Barrenness, leanness, and sterility have seized upon all the fields of man's tillage. They yield him nothing. He sows, but he reaps not; he plows, but obtains no harvest. By the works of the flesh no man living can be justified, and in the devices of human tradition or human reason, no souls can possibly find substantial comfort. See you, disciples of Christ, see you the great need which is before your eyes. Open the eyes of your understanding now, let your bowels move, let your hearts beat with sympathy, let your souls be alive to pity – do feel for those millions! I implore you, if you cannot help them, weep over them; let there be now before your mind's eye a clear and distinct recognition of the many hundreds and thousands who are crying to you, "Feed us, for we famish; give us bread to eat, or we die."

I think I hear you reason in your hearts and whisper one to another, "Who are we that we should feed this multitude? Look at their hosts, who can count them? As the stars of heaven for multitude, so are the seed of Adam. These hungry, craving mouths are almost as numerous as the sands on the seashore; what do we have that we should give them to eat?" Even so. Yet, remember, this is your mission. Neither do any of you do well to take up and adopt a weakness of faith that was illustrated by Philip's questioning. If ever the world is to be led, it is with Christ through the church. Until the kingdoms of the world become the kingdoms of our Lord and of his Christ, we are the warriors who must carry the victorious arms of the cross to the uttermost parts of the earth. We are the social-service workers of God's free generosity, until the fullness of the Gentiles is gathered in. God commands all men everywhere to repent; and we are to utter his mandate.

> **By the works of the flesh no man living can be justified.**

Oh, my brethren, you know how Jesus worked the work of his Father; you know how he went about doing good; but do you know how he said, *"Greater works than these he will do; because I go to the Father"*? Let the words sink down into your ears. Let the vision rise perpetually before your eyes. See your work. Great as it is, dispirited as you may be by the great multitude who crave your help, yet recognize the appeal to your faith. Let the magnitude of the mission drive you the more earnestly to the work instead of deterring you from it.

Do I hear you murmur, "The multitudes are great, and sparse is the supply. We have but five loaves, and they are made of barley; we have but two fish, and they are little ones. The bread hardly suffices for ourselves; the fish are so small that they will be more bones than meat. What are these among so many? So I hear you tell us, sir, that we as a church are to feed the world; how can we? How few are our talents! We are not rich in substance; we have no wealth with which to supply our missionaries, that we may send them out by hosts to lift up the banner of Christ. We have little talent; there are not many among us who are learned or wise; we have not much eloquence. We feel, though we do not feel enough:

> Fain my pity would reclaim,
> And snatch the firebrand from the flame;
> But feeble my compassion proves,
> And fain must weep where most it loves."

"Besides," some of you add, "what can I do individually? Of what use can I be? And what can the few friends who are in earnest do? Why, the world will laugh at such a feeble body of men. They will say, 'What can these feeble Jews do?' We have a mountain before us, and we have to level it to a plain – how can we do it? Our strength is not sufficient; we are destitute of power. Oh, if we only had the great and noble on our side! If we only had kings to be the nursing fathers, and queens the nursing mothers of our church! If we only had the rich to give their lavish treasure, and the learned to give their wit, and the eloquent to give their golden speech, then we *might* succeed! But alas! alas! silver and gold have we none; and at the Master's feet we can lay but little: so little that it is utterly insignificant when compared with the world's languishing needs, the whole creation's pitiful laboring groans."

Then I think I hear you heave a sigh and say again, "There is no more that we know of, no more bread that is procurable; we cannot buy for all this multitude." If we have little gifts ourselves, we cannot buy the eloquence of others. Indeed, it would be of no use if it were bought, for eloquent speech purchased is of no use to any cause. We need for Christ's cause the free utterance of willing men who "speak through their throats," and feel from their hearts what they propound with their lips. Such speak because they cannot help speaking. *For woe is me if I do not preach the gospel.* If we have little ability of our own, we cannot buy more of others. The offices of love can never be delegated to the worker. But I think I hear your disheartened spirits crying, "If we could add mercenary troops to the host of God, we might succeed; if we could procure by our donations more help, more strength for the Lord God of Hosts, then there might be bread in his house, and then the multitudes might be fed." But two hundred pennyworths would not suffice for the five thousand, and millions would not suffice for the thousand millions of poor unenlightened men and women. Master, what can we do? There are so many; we have not the bread ourselves, and we cannot buy it on their behalf.

And then I hear the groan of one who is growing gray in years: "Oh! I feel it, but it is getting late with me, and the world's necessities are getting stern; the hunger has continued until men are famished; they have been without bread till they are ready to perish and faint by the way, and the night comes on, a long and dreary night – who shall work then? We are ready to go down into our graves; our shadows are lengthened and our frame is shrunken; we are weak, and we hang our heads like bulrushes, as men who seek the grave that has long been seeking them." Let me tell you, brethren and fathers, we who are in our opening youth, we feel that too. Good God! our days spin around us now, and our weeks seem to be hissing through the air, leaving a track like that of a burning brand.

Work as we may, and some of us can say that we lose no time in Christ's cause, yet we can do nothing. We seem to be like one man alone against an innumerable host, or like a child seeking to remove a mountain with its own puny hand. Night is getting spent, we are growing withered, our years are flying by, our deaths are coming on. Souls are dying, hell is filling. Down the waterfall of destruction men are being plunged incessantly beyond our sight, beyond our hope. We cannot do it. The more we feel our responsibility, the more our infirmity oppresses us. You have called us to a work that is too hard. We cannot do it, Master. We come to your feet, and we say we cannot give these multitudes to eat. Mock us not. Command us not to do impossibilities. You have bidden us to preach the gospel to every creature under heaven. We cannot reach them. We are too few; we are too feeble; we are too weak; we are too devoid of talent. Master, we cannot do it. At your feet we are ready to fall in sheer despair.

But hark! I hear the cries of the multitude as they come up in our ears. They say to us, "We are perishing; will you let us perish? We are famishing; will you let us famish? Our fathers have gone down to hell, and our fathers' fathers have perished for lack of the bread that came down from heaven, and will you let us die?" Across from Africa the multitudes look over the sea to us, and they beckon with their fingers – "Will you let us perish? Shall we forever be hunting ground for those who delight in chains and bloodshed?" From Asia they lift up the cry, "Will you always leave us? Shall we always be the bondslaves of Juggernaut, Brahma, Servia, and Vishnu?" From Australia they cry to us, such as have not already perished; the Aborigines cry, "Shall we never see the light? Shall we never hear the gospel?" And worse than the Aborigines, the wail of not a few who remember in night-dreams the services of our sanctuaries, but have forgotten in their day labors the observance of our Sabbaths, their cry is piercing indeed. Oh! how terrible is the wail – the combined wail that comes up from all the nations under heaven!

One man in Paul's dream who said, "Come over and help us!" was enough to constrain him; and here are millions not in a dream, but in open vision, who all at once say, "Come and help us." Did we say, just now, that we could not? Surely we must recall our words and say, "We must." Good Master, we must! If we cannot, we must. We feel our weakness, but there is an impulse within us that says we must do it, and we cannot stop, we dare not – we would be accursed if we did. The blasts of hell and the wrath of heaven would fall upon us if we renounced the task. The world's only hope – shall we put that out? The lone star that covers the darkness with gold – shall we quench that? The Savior of men, and shall we fold our arms and let them die? No! by the love we bear your name; by the bonds that unite us to you; by everything that is holy before God and humane in the sight of our fellow mortals; by everything that is tender and gentle in the throbbing of our hearts and the yearning of our bowels, we say we must, though we feel we cannot.

Yet there is a strong tendency in our hearts to shift personal responsibility. "Let us send them away into the villages to buy meat." We look towards some Bethsaida in the distance, and say, "Let them go there and get good." This is a strong temptation with many churches. Perhaps you say, "We have not got all this work to do; there are other churches, let them do their part. In all the suburbs of London there are chapels. There is the parish church; can they not hear the gospel there? There is the city missionary going about after them; what need is there that we should visit them? No doubt there are some good men preaching in the street; what necessity is it that I should do it? Let them go into the villages and get meat." Ah, but not so. The Master said to you, *"You give them something to eat!"* *"You."* Let this church feel that it should look upon the world as if it were the only church, and do its utmost as if it had no helper under heaven, but had all the work to do by itself. And let the entire body of the church of our Lord Jesus Christ – instead of looking to societies for evangelization, or to commerce, or to governments – remember that she is the sole savior of the world.

Christ never was incarnate in kings and in princes. His incarnation today is in the sacramental host of his elect. If you ask me where was God on earth, I point to the man Christ Jesus. If you ask me where is Christ on earth, I point you to his faithful church, called by his Spirit. As Christ was the world's hope, so is the church the world's hope, and she must take up the charge as if there were not another. Instead of sending some to this town and some to that, she must hear her Master say, *"You give them something to eat!"*

I do fear, dear friends, that many of us are getting into a very easy state about perishing men, because we keep out of their way. To stop your ears to the cries of the hungry, or shut your eyes to the needs of the widow and the fatherless is not the way to relieve famine. Nor is it the way of doing good in the world, to avoid the stomping grounds of the poor, and to leave the dens of desolation and sin. It is ours to touch the leper with our healing finger, not to shrink from his presence; it is ours to go and find out the stripped, and wounded, and helpless of the sons of men, and then to pour on the oil and the wine. Leave the priest and the Levite, if they will, to pass by on the other side. Your Master asks of you, Christian, practical, personal service, and your Christianity is worth nothing unless it makes you heed his word – *"You give them something to eat!"* Unless it makes you as individual members, and as a united body, do God's work for the world's sake and for Jesus Christ's sake, I will tell you, the people of my charge, that the world's salvation is given instrumentally into your hands. As far as your power lies, you are to consider yourselves as the world's hope, and you are to act as such. And what shall I say of you if, instead of accepting this charge from Christ, you sit still and do nothing?

If, after having built this ceilinged house in which you meet, you should disregard others who hear not the Word of Christ – if, being fed with heaven's food yourselves, you shall be satisfied to let others perish, I tell you that as a church, "regret" shall be written upon your brow. The garments of this church shall be torn, and her veil shall be torn away from her. She shall be set as a sign of disapproval; she shall be made a pillar of salt, like Lot's wife, throughout all generations, if she dares to look back now that the Master has called her to a great and solemn work. He that puts his hand to the plow and looks back is not worthy of the kingdom. I have faith in you, dear friends, but I have more faith in my God; I have faith in you that you will not turn back, but accept the exceedingly great charge which comes upon you of giving light to the world. But if you reject it, I will be a swift witness against you at the last great day, that you knew your Master's will and that you did not do it – that you were called to the Master's service and you slunk back again to laziness and sloth.

Having thus dwelt upon our mission, and enlarged upon our weakness, it is time to turn the topic and come to our line of duty and the Master's strength.

Our line of duty begins, first of all, in immediate obedience to Christ's first command – *"Bring them here to Me."* "Five loaves, Master, it is all we have, and two fish." *"Bring them here to Me."* In Mark, the words are used – *"Go look!"* They were to look in their wallets and be quite sure that they had not anything more. They were to rummage among all their treasures, and bring every crust, every piece of flesh, or bread, to Christ. *"Bring them here to Me."* "Master, they are barley loaves; only five." *"Bring them here to Me."* "There are two fish; they are only two; they are not worth thinking of; let us keep them for ourselves." "No, bring them to me." "But they are such little fish." *"Bring them here to Me,"* says he, *"bring them here to Me."*

The church's first duty is, when she looks to her resources and feels them to be utterly insufficient for her work, to still bring all that she has to Christ. But how shall she bring them? Why, in many ways. She must bring them to Christ *in consecration*. There is a brother yonder who says, "Well, I have but little money to spare!" "Never mind," says Christ. "Let what you have be brought to me." "Ah," says another, "I have very short time that I can spare in laboring to do good." "Bring it to me." "Ah," says another, "but I have small ability; my stock of knowledge is very slender; my speech is contemptible." "Bring it to me." "Oh," says one, "I could only teach in the Sunday school." "Bring it to me." "Ah," says another, "and I do not know that I could do that; I could only distribute a tract." "Bring it to me." Every talent that the church has is to be brought to Christ and consecrated. And mark you this – I speak a strong thing which some will not be able to receive – anything which you have in this world, which you do not consecrate to Christ's cause, you rob the Lord of.

Every true Christian, when he gave himself to Christ, gave everything he had. Neither does he call anything that he has his own, but it is all the Master's. We are not true to the Master's cause unless it be so. "What! not provide for our families?" Yes, truly, but that is given to God. "Not provide for ourselves?" Yes, truly, so long as you are not covetous. Remember, it is your Master's business to provide for you. If he provides for you through your own exertions, you are doing your Master's work and receiving from his generosity, for it is his work to provide for you. But still there must always be a thorough consecration of everything you have to Christ. Where your consecration ends, your honesty with God ends. How often you have made the vow in your hymn! And will you not be true to your covenant with him?

"All that I am, and all I have,
    Shall be for ever thine;
Whate'er my duty bids me give,
    My cheerful hands resign."

"And if I might make some reserve,
    And duty did not call,
I love my God with zeal so great,
    That I would give him all."

Bring them to me – not only in consecration, but also in prayer. I think our prayer-meetings should be the seasons when the church brings up all her barley loaves and fish to Christ. To get them blessed, here we come together, great Master, around the altar. We are weak and feeble, we come to be made strong; we have no power of ourselves; we come that we may receive power from on high; and we wait in the prayer meeting, as your disciples did in the upper room at Jerusalem, till the Spirit be poured out. It is marvelous how a man with one talent can sometimes do ten times more than a man with ten talents, for he has ten times the grace.

    A soldier, after all, is not always useful according to his weapon. Give a fool an Armstrong gun, and perhaps he will destroy himself with it. Give a wise man only the poorest piece of firearms, and you shall find, with good and steady aim and bold advance, that he shall do more service with his small weapons than the other with far better arms. So there are men, who seem as if they might be leaders in God's house, that are dawdlers, doing nothing, while there are others who are but little in Israel, whom God through his grace makes to be mighty. Bring to this place, O you servants of the Lord, all that you have kept back; pour all the tithes into his storehouse, that his house may be full. *"Test Me now in this,"* says the Lord of hosts, *"if I will not open for you the windows of heaven and pour out for you a blessing until it overflows."*

    Let us bring all we have to Christ, likewise in faith, laying it all at his feet, believing that his great power can make little means suffice for mighty ends. "Lord, there are only five loaves" – they were five loaves only when we had them in our hands, but now they are in your hands; they are food for five thousand men. "Lord, there are two fish" – they were inferior to insignificance while they were ours, but your touch has ennobled them, and those little fish shall become food for that vast multitude.

Blessed is that man who, feeling that he has truly consecrated all to God, can say, "There is enough. I do not want more talent; I do not need more substance; I would not wish to have more, there is enough for my work; I know it is utterly insufficient in itself, but our sufficiency is in God." Oh! do not tell me, sirs, that we, as a denomination, are too feeble to do much good. Do not tell me that the Christianity of England is too weak for the evangelization of the whole world. No such thing; there is enough, there is plenty, if the Master satisfies it. If there were only six good men living, and these six were thoroughly consecrated to God, they would be enough for the world's conversion. It is not the multiplication of your means; it is not the complication of your machinery; it is not the organization of your societies; it is not the qualification of your secretaries that God cares about one bit – it is your consecrated men who are wholly his and only his. Let them believe that he can make them mighty, and they shall be mighty through God to the pulling down of strongholds.

I do not hesitate to say that there are some pulpits that would be better empty than occupied; that there are some congregations to whom it would be far better if they had no preacher at all; for, having a minister who is not ordained of God, and not speaking by faith, they content themselves with things as they are, and grow listless. If the hoax were taken away, they might cry out for a real ministry. God would bestow on them one taught of the Holy Spirit, who would speak with a tongue of fire, with inward witness and with spiritual energy, resting his confidence in God's promises and his Word. Dear friends, we ought to believe that there is enough means if Christ does but bless them, enough to bring in God's chosen ones.

"Bring them here to Me," once more, in active service. That which is dedicated to Christ in solemn covenant, and in earnest prayer, and in humble faith, must be dedicated in active service. Are you *all* at work for Christ? Members of this church, I speak to you first; it is

but incidentally that I address other believers here. Are you all doing something for Christ? I think there should not be a single member of this church who is not somehow occupied for the Master. Shall I make an exception for any? – except the weak upon their beds, and they can speak a good word for him when they are visited; except the dying upon their couches, and they can bear a blessed testimony to his faithfulness when they are going through the river; except the dumb, and they can act out religion, when they cannot speak it; except the blind, and they can sing his praises; except the utterly incapacitated, and these can magnify the Lord by their patience. Still we ought, every one of us, if we be Christ's, to be serving him. Am I a son, and have I no duty to my father? Am I a husband, and have I no duties of kindness to my wife? Am I a servant, and shall I be idle, careless, and disobedient? Is the Christian's the only name that is merely nominal? Is this a barren title? Is this a medal to be worn? Is this a kind of cross which Christians shall take when they have done no deeds of arms, no valiant conflicts for Christ? Is the Christian only a thing, and not a living reality? The Lord have mercy upon such Christians!

Now, dear friends, if you want any inducements to lead you to bring all that you have to Christ, let me urge this. In bringing it to him, you put your talent into *his* hand, whose hand was pierced for you. You give to him who is your dearest friend; you give to him who spared not the blood of his heart that he might redeem you. Do you not love him? Is it not an honor to be permitted to show your love to so notable and noble a person? We have heard of women that have worked, and all but starved themselves, to bring food for their children; and as they put the precious morsels into the little ones' mouths, they felt their toil to be nothing, because they were giving it to those they loved. And so with the believer – he should feel that he most blesses himself when he blesses Christ. And, indeed, when the Christian does a duty for Jesus, it more blesses him that gives than him that takes.

> The believer should feel that he most blesses himself when he blesses Christ.

Besides, when you give to him, you have another inducement, that you are thus giving to the multitude. I know people think, when they are doing something for the church, that they are pleasing the minister, or pleasing the deacons. Oh! dear friends, it is not so. What interest have I in all the world but the love of poor souls – that God who reads the heart shall say, at the day of judgment, there lives not one who desires more freely from selfish motive the salvation of this world than the minister who addresses you now. And I trust I can speak the same of my brethren in Christ who long to see the world brought in. Look at that hungry world, and when you give the bread, let those eyes that stare upon you, let those who eat so abundantly thank you, and let that be a sufficient recompense for what you have done.

There is a man, I think, present now, who I remember, some two or three winters ago, came to me to join the church. When I sat down in the room to talk to him, I saw by the look on the poor man's face that he wanted natural bread as well as spiritual bread. So I said, "Before I talk to you, I would like to see you a little refreshed," and we fetched him something to eat. I looked at him for a minute, for I saw his eyes glisten, and I left the room, for fear he would not eat so much when I was there. This, though, I can tell you, that when I saw the great pleasure with which he ate, it would have been sufficient compensation to me even if that little bit of food had cost ten thousand pounds. And when you see the poor sinner lay hold of Christ so greedily, and yet so joyfully, when you see his gleaming eye, and the tear as it runs down his cheek, you will say, "I am too well paid to have done good to such a poor heart as this. Lord, it is enough, I have fed these hungry souls."

Once again, bring your loaves and fish to Christ instead of following Christ to get loaves and fish. Is it no inducement that you should yourself be the distributor? When we were children, and our father cut off a small piece from the meat, and sent it to a sick woman down the road, do we not recollect how Thomas, Mary, and Ann used to quarrel for turns to take the basin over to her with the slice of meat? We always liked to knock at the good woman's door and say, "Please, we have brought something for your dinner today." Children are always glad if there is something to give away. If you put a penny into their hands to give to a poor blind man, how cheerfully they run! Just such a feeling as that the Christian has when out of his talent, which he has consecrated to God, he does something for the world. He is going about among the ranks, and feeding them, and he has joy in the deed.

Then to close this point. *"Bring them here to Me,* and you shall have as much left as you had when you brought them." They took up of the fragments more than ever they gave. Christ will never let any man die in his debt. What you have done unto him is abundantly repaid, if not in worldly things, yet in spiritual things. The fragments shall fill the baskets that are so liberally emptied. You shall find that while watering others you are yourself watered. The joy you impart shall be mutual. To do good is to get good, and to distribute to others for Christ is the surest way of enriching one's self.

The rest of the believer's duty I will briefly sum up. When you have brought your talents to Christ, and have a conscientiousness of your great mission, your next duty is to look up. Thank God for what you have got; look up! Say, "There is nothing in what I do; there is nothing in my prayers, my preaching, my actions, my doings, except you bless the whole. Lord, bless it!" Then, when you have blessed, break. Remember the multiplication never came till after the division, and the addition did not begin till the subtraction took place. So then, begin to break, do good, and communicate. Go abroad, and actively serve the Master, and when you have thus broken and have thus distributed to others, remember that you only distribute from Christ's own hand. You are to put your talents and abilities into Christ's hand. He gives the blessing on it; then he gives back to you, and afterwards, you give it to the people. If I give you bread from this pulpit to eat that is my own, it will be of no use to you. But if, having gotten it in my study, I put it in the hand of Christ, and come up here, and Christ hands it back to me, and I give it to you, then you shall be fed to the full. This is Christ's way of blessing men; he does not give the blessing first to the world, but to his disciples, and then the disciples give it to the multitude. We get in private what we distribute in public. We have access to God as his chosen favorites. We come near to him. He gives to us, we give to others.

Thus, dear friends, I began by setting before you a great and high mission. First, I made you say, "We cannot"; then I tried to make you say, "We must." And now I want to end by making you say, "We can."

> **You are to put your talents into Christ's hand. He gives the blessing on it; then he gives back to you, and afterwards, you give it to the people.**

Yes! Christ is with us, and we can. God is for us, and we can. The Holy Spirit is in us, and we can. God the Holy Spirit calls us; Jesus Christ the Son of God cheers us; God the Father smiles upon us; we can, we must, we will. The kingdoms of this world shall become the kingdoms of our Lord and of his Christ.

But have we believed in Christ ourselves? If not, we can do nothing. Come to Jesus first, then work for Jesus. Give him your own heart first, then give him all that you have. So shall he accept your offering and bless your soul for his name's sake.

Chapter 8

Jesus Knew What He Would Do

This He was saying to test him, for He Himself knew what He was intending to do. (John 6:6)

Observe, dear friends, how careful the Holy Spirit is that we should not make a mistake about our Lord Jesus Christ. He knew that men are liable to think too little of the ever-blessed Son of God, and that some, who call themselves Christians, nevertheless deny Christ's divinity, and are ever ready to forge an argument against the true and real deity of the Savior out of anything which appears to limit his power or knowledge. Here is an instance of the care of the Spirit to prevent our falling into an erroneous conclusion. Our Lord consults with Philip, asking this poor disciple, *"Where are we to buy bread, so that these may eat?"* Some might therefore have inferred that Jesus did not know what to do, but felt embarrassed. From this they would argue that Jesus cannot be almighty God, for surely embarrassment is inconsistent with Omnipotence. Why should Jesus consult with Philip if he knows all things?

Now, the Holy Spirit would have us beware of falling into low thoughts of our great Redeemer and Lord, and especially of ever being so mistaken as to think that he is not God; therefore, he plainly tells us, *This He was saying to test him, for He Himself knew what He was intending to do.* Jesus was not asking for information or taking counsel with

Philip because he felt any doubt about his line of procedure, or needed help from his disciple. He did not want Philip to multiply bread, but he desired to multiply Philip's faith. Take heed, therefore, dear friends, that you never think little of the Savior, or credit any of his acts to motives that would lessen his glory.

Learn here, too, that we, being very apt to make mistakes concerning Christ, need daily that the Spirit of God should interpret Christ to us. Jesus simply asks the question of Philip, *"Where are we to buy bread?"* and we are at once in danger of drawing a wrong inference, and therefore the Holy Spirit tells us more about Christ so that we may escape from that danger. By giving us more insight into our Lord's motives, he prevents our misjudging his actions. We must have the Spirit of God with us, or we will not know Christ himself. The only way to see the sun is by its own light; and the only way to see Jesus is by his own Spirit. Did he not himself say, *"He will take of Mine and will disclose it to you"*? No man can call Jesus "Lord" but by the Holy Spirit. The Spirit must come to each man personally, and reveal the Son of God to him and in him.

Therefore, do not let us take up the Bible and imagine that we shall at once understand it as we do another book, but let us breathe the prayer that the Great Author of its letter would himself give us grace to enter into its spirit, so as to know its meaning and feel its power. Even with the infallible Word before you, you will miss your way and fall into grievous error unless you are taught of God. The mercy is that it is written, *"All your sons will be taught of the Lord";* and again, *You have an anointing from the Holy One, and you all know.* There is no knowing anything except by that anointing and by that divine teaching. What dependent creatures we are, since we make mistakes even about Jesus Christ himself unless the Spirit of God is pleased to instruct us concerning him! Lead us ever, O light of God!

Another thing we learn from the text before we plunge into it is that our divine Lord always has a reason for everything that he does. Even the reason for his asking a question may be found out; or, if we cannot discover it, we may still be quite sure that there is a worthy reason. That

> The only way to see the sun is by its own light; and the only way to see Jesus is by his own Spirit.

reason in Philip's case certainly was not because of any lack of wisdom in himself, but there was a reason – *This He was saying to test him.* Now, if there is a reason for all that Jesus asks, much more is there a reason for all that he does. We cannot tell the reason for election – why this man is chosen or that man; but there is a reason, since God never acts unreasonably, though his reasons are not always revealed, and might not be understood by us if they were. Sovereignty is absolute, but it is never absurd. There is always a justifiable cause for all that God does in the kingdom of grace, though that cause is not the merit of the person whom he favors, for merit there is none.

In the matter of your present trial and trouble, dear friend, you have been trying to spell out the design of the Almighty, but without success. Know you not that his ways are past finding out? In all probability this side of eternity you may never discover God's purpose in your present trial, but that he has a purpose is certain, and that purpose is a wise and kind one. It is such as you yourself would delight in if you were capable of understanding it. If you could have a mind like that of God, you would act as God does even in this matter which troubles you; at present your thoughts are far below those of God, and therefore you err when you try to measure his ways. If you have a quarrel with your heavenly Father about a bereavement or a sickness, end it at once with humble shame. There, child, if it ever comes to a question as to which is right – a poor, ignorant, and inexperienced youth, or a great, good, and wise Father – there cannot be a moment's deliberation; the Father's will must be better for the child than its own will. Be in subjection to the Father of spirits and live. Do believe in your Lord, and be quieted; Jesus knows what he is doing and why he is doing it.

For the loss of your health there is a reason. For those pains of body, for that depression of spirit, for that lack of success in business, even for the permission of the cruel tongue of slander to inflict its wounds upon you, there is a reason, and possibly that reason may lie in the words of our text: *This He was saying to test him.* You must be tested. God does not give faith, or love, or hope, or any grace without meaning to prove it. If a man builds a railway bridge, it is so that engines may go over it, so that its carrying power may be proved. If a man makes a road, it is so that there may be traffic over it; every rod of it will be proved by wheels and hoofs. If he only makes a needle, it must be tested by the work it can do. When the pillars that now support these galleries were cast, they were made with the object of supporting a great weight, and these twenty years they have bravely endured the pressure. It would have been an idle thing to have set them up and placed no weight upon them.

So when God made you, my brother, to be strong in the Lord, he meant to test every ounce of your strength; for that which God makes has a purpose, and he will prove it to see that it is equal to its design. I do not think that a single grain of faith will be kept out of the fire; all the golden ore must go into the crucible to be tested. You have heard of the Birmingham proving houses for the barrels of guns; now, the great Maker of believers proves all whom he makes in his factory of grace with heavy charges of affliction, and only those that can bear the test shall receive his mark. When no other explanation of a providence can be found, you may always fall back upon the belief that this he said and this he did to prove you.

Let us at once come to the text, which seems to me to have much comfort in it. May the Holy Spirit lead us into it.

First, here is *a question for Philip* – "Where are we to buy bread, so that these may eat?" – a question with a purpose. But secondly, there is *no question with the Master,* for he himself knew what he would do. And thirdly, if we enter into the spirit of the Master there will be *an end of questions with us,* for we shall be perfectly satisfied that he knows what he is going to do.

First, then, here is a question for Philip, as there have been many questions for us. Jesus put this question to Philip *with the motive of proving him* in several points. He would thus test his faith. As one has well said, "He wanted not food from Philip, but faith." The Master asks, *"Where are we to buy bread, so that these may eat?"* What will Philip say? If Philip has strong faith he will answer, "Great Master, there is no need to buy bread; you are greater than Moses, and under Moses the people were fed with manna in the wilderness. You have only to speak the word, and bread shall be rained around the host, and they shall be filled." If Philip had possessed great faith he might have replied, "You are greater than Elisha, and Elisha took a few loaves and ears of corn and fed the sons of the prophets. O wonder-working Lord, you can do the same." If Philip had displayed greater faith still, he might have said, "Lord, I do not know where bread is to be bought, but it is written, *'Man shall not live on bread alone.'* You can refresh these people without visible bread. You can satisfy their hunger and fill them to the full, and yet they need not eat a single mouthful, for it is written, *'But on every word that proceeds out of the mouth of God* shall man live.' Speak the word, and they will be at once refreshed."

This question, therefore, was put to prove Philip's faith. It did prove it, and proved it to be very little, for he began calculating his pennyworths – "One, two, three, four." No, I will not count to two hundred, but that is what Philip did. He began counting pennies instead of looking to Omnipotence. Did you ever do the same, dear friend, when you have been tested? Did you get reckoning up and counting copper coins instead of looking to the eternal God and trusting in him? I fear that few of us can plead exemption from this failure, since even Moses once fell into unbelieving calculations. *But Moses said, "The people, among whom I am, are 600,000 on foot; yet You have said, 'I will give them meat, so that they may eat for a whole month.' Should flocks and herds be slaughtered for them, to be sufficient for them? Or should all the fish of the sea be gathered together for them, to be sufficient for them?"* Remember God's answer to his anxious servant: *The Lord said to Moses, "Is the Lord's power limited? Now you shall see whether My word will come true for you or not."* Even so shall we see the faithfulness of God, but if we are unbelieving, we may have to see it in a way which will painfully bring home to us our sin in having distrusted our Lord.

The question was meant, no doubt, to prove Philip's love, and he could endure that test better than he could stand the other; for he loved Jesus even though he was slow of heart to believe. In many true hearts there is more quiet love than active faith. I am sorry that there should be little faith, but am thankful that there should be more love. The Savior seemed to say, "Philip, I want these people to be fed. Will you come to my aid in it? Where shall *we* buy bread? I am going to associate you with me, Philip. Come, now, how shall *we* do the work?" Philip loves his Master, and therefore he is quite ready to consider the matter, and to give at least the benefit of his arithmetic. He says, *"Two hundred denarii worth of bread is not sufficient for them."* His Master did not ask him what would *not* be sufficient, but what *would* be; but Philip begins calculating the negative question – which question I also am afraid that you and I have often calculated. Even to give each one in the crowd a little could not be done for less than two hundred pence; is it not clear that our resources are inadequate? That is always a depressing and unpractical question to go into. Poor Philip counts up what would *not* be sufficient for all, and leaves the all-sufficient Lord out of the reckoning. Still, even in that calculation he showed his love for his Master. If he had not been full of love and esteem for Jesus he would have said, "My Lord, it is idle to go into that. We are a poor group of people. We have a small sum of money given to us every now and then, and I do not quite know how it goes, perhaps Judas does; but I am persuaded that there is not enough in the bag to feed these multitudes, even if there were bakers' shops in the neighborhood at which we could buy loaves."

But Philip did not answer this way. No, he had too much reverence and too much love for Jesus for that; he failed in his faith, but he did not fail in his love. It will be well for us to love our Lord so much that we never speak of his gracious plans as being visionary, nor judge them to be impossible. Jesus never proposes foolishly impractical schemes, and we must never allow the idea to cross our minds. Even the conquest of the world to truth and righteousness is not to be looked upon as a dream, but to be practically considered.

The question also tested Philip's *sympathy.* Jesus by this query moved Philip's heart to care about the people. The other disciples said, *"Send the crowds away, that they may go into the villages and buy food for themselves."* Jesus, perhaps noticing a little more tenderness in Philip than in the others, said to Philip, *"Where are we to buy bread?"* It was putting great honor upon Philip to associate him with himself, but perhaps he saw in him a sympathetic soul, and Christ loves to work with sympathetic agents.

One thing I notice – that God seldom uses greatly a man who has a hard heart or a cold heart. Warmth within ourselves can alone create warmth in others. A man must love people or he cannot save them. A minister must have an intense desire that his congregation should be saved, and must get into sympathy with Jesus upon that subject, or else Jesus will not make use of him. So our Lord sought to stir up Philip's sympathy. "Come, Philip, what shall you and I do? Where shall *we* buy bread to give them to eat?" I do not think Philip failed altogether there. He had not such sympathy with his Master as he ought to have had, but he had a measure of it. I trust that our God has given to us also some communion with his dear Son in his love for the souls of men, and so this question comes to prove us.

Let us not be lacking either in faith, or love, or sympathy. God grant that we may abound in all these through the effectual working of his Holy Spirit; then shall we be fitted to be workers together with him.

But why was that question put *to Philip*? Why is a special question put to some one of you, or a peculiar trial sent to one of you? It was sent to test him, it is said; but why to test *Philip*?

Well, I think the Savior spoke to Philip because Philip was from Bethsaida. They were near Bethsaida, and so Jesus said to Philip, *"Where are we to buy bread?"* Every man should think most of the place where he lives. I want Jesus to say to some of you, "What shall we do for London?" – because many of you are Londoners – possibly born within the sound of Bow bells, or within the postal district. You belong to the four million of this great province – no, this great nation, of a city, and it is a solemn responsibility to be a citizen of the greatest city in the world. If the Lord does lay London on anybody's hearts, he would naturally lay it upon the hearts of those who live in it, just as he said to Philip, *"Where are we to buy bread?"* If he associates anybody with himself in the evangelization of a village or town, it will naturally be a person either born there or living there.

I know that the old proverb declares that the cobbler's wife goes barefoot, and sometimes a man will care for people thousands of miles away, and not look to his own house or to his own neighborhood. But it should not be so, for it is to Philip, the Bethsaida man, that the message comes about the people when they are near Bethsaida – *"Where are we to buy bread?"* It is said to test him; and to you, brother Londoner, questions about this great city are sent to test you.

It is also probable that it was Philip's department to attend to the providing for the little company of twelve and their Leader. Judas was the treasurer, and, unless we are much mistaken, Philip was the butler. It was Philip's business to see that they had bread in the traveling bag, and his part to make some little provision when the band of disciples went into desert places. Even so, there are brethren here present whose official business it is to care for the souls of men. Among these are ministers, missionaries, Sunday school teachers, deacons, elders, district visitors, Bible women, and the like. If the Lord does not say to others, "What shall we do for London?" he says it to us. The question is sent to test us as to whether we are fit for our office, or whether we have taken upon ourselves a position for which we are not qualified because we have no heart for it. Christ asks *us* especially, but I think he also asks all those whom he has made priests and kings unto God, "*Where are we to buy bread?* How shall we feed this great city?" The question comes to test us because it is upon us that this burden ought to be laid.

And perhaps it came to Philip because he was not quite so forward in the school of grace as some were. Philip did not make a very wise remark when he said, "*Lord, show us the Father, and it is enough for us,*" for our Lord answered, "*Have I been so long with you, and yet you have not come to know Me, Philip?*" He was evidently slow in learning. I do not think that Philip was the most stupid of the twelve, but I am sure that he was not the most intelligent. James and John and Peter were the first three; Andrew and Thomas followed close behind, and probably Philip was close after them. Perhaps Philip was number six, I do not know; but certainly the Savior selected him as not the lowest in the class, yet not the highest either, and he said to him, "*Where are we to buy bread?*" These people in the middle position very much need testing for their own satisfaction. The lowest kind of Christians are so feeble that they can hardly bear testing. Poor souls, they need encouraging rather than testing, and therefore the greatest problems are not often pressed upon them.

On the other hand, the highest kind of Christians do not so much require testing, for they make their calling and election sure. The middle sort most need testing, and they make up, I am afraid, the great bulk of the rank and file of the army of God. How many there are who may be described as half instructed, half enlightened, and to these the Lord puts the question, *"Where are we to buy bread?"* This he says so that he may test them.

Note well that *the question which the Savior put to Philip to test him answered its purpose.* It did test him. How it tested him I have shown you already. It answered its purpose because it revealed his inability. *"Where are we to buy bread?"* Philip gives it up. He has made a calculation of what would *not* suffice even to give every man a little refreshment, and that is all his contribution to the work; he has not even a loaf or a fish which he can produce to make a start with. Philip is beaten. What is more, his faith, being tested, is beaten too. "Oh, good Master," he seems to say, "the people cannot be fed by us. *We* cannot buy bread – we – not even you and I. You are the Lord, and you can do great things; yet my faith is not strong enough to believe that *we* could buy bread enough for all these thousands of people." So the question answered its purpose. It tested Philip's faith, and his faith was proved to be very weak, very wavering, very shorthanded. Is it a good thing to find that out?

Yes, brethren, it is good to know our spiritual poverty. Many of us have a heap of faith, as we think, but if the Lord were to test it, he would not need to put it *in* the fire to melt it; he has only to put it *on* the fire, and most of it would evaporate. Under ordinary trials, much faith disappears like morning dew when the sun looks upon it. What a deal of faith a man has when he is healthy! Just turn on the screw and let him suffer. See how much of that faith will vanish. How many men have faith if they have an excellent income regularly paid; but when they have to ask, "Where will the next meal come from?" have they faith? Alas, they grow anxious and burdened. It is a wholesome thing to be made to see what weaklings we are, for when we find much of our faith to be unreal, it drives us to seek for more true faith, and we cry, "Lord, increase our faith!"

> **What a deal of faith a man has when he is healthy!**

Philip was drawn into his Master; and it is a grand thing to be driven right out of ourselves to our Lord so as to feel, "Lord, I cannot do it; but I long to see how you will perform your purpose. I cannot even believe in you as I ought to believe, unless you give me faith, so that even for more faith I must come to you. Quite empty-handed I must come and borrow everything." Then it is that we become full and strong. You will see Philip breaking the bread directly, and feeding the multitude just because Christ has emptied Philip's hands. Until he has emptied our hands he cannot fill them, lest it should be supposed that we shared in the supplying. *This He was saying to test him,* to make him see his own weakness, for then he would be filled with the Master's strength.

This question did good, for *it was meant not only to test Philip but to also test the other disciples,* and so they came together, and they had a little talk upon the subject. At any rate, here is a committee of two – Philip and Andrew. Philip says, *"Two hundred denarii worth of bread is not sufficient for them,"* and Andrew says, "Well, no, it is not; but there is a lad here with five barley loaves and two small fish." I like this brotherly consultation of willing minds, and to see how they differ in their ideas. Philip is willing to begin if he has a grand start; he must see at least two hundred denarii worth of bread in hand, and then he is ready to entertain the idea. Andrew, on the other hand, is willing to begin with a small amount; a few loaves and fish will enable him to start, but he remarks, *"What are these for so many people?"* When saints converse together they help each other, and perhaps what one does not discover another may. Philip was counting the impossible pennies, and could not see the possible loaves, but Andrew could see what Philip overlooked. He spied out the lad with that basket packed full of loaves and fish. It was not much: Andrew had not faith enough to see food for the thousands in that little basket; but still he saw what he did see, and he told the Master of it.

Thus they made a beginning by mutual consultation; perhaps if we were to consult we might make a start too. When a question eats into men's hearts like this – "What shall we do for London?" when it leads Christian people to come together and talk about it, and when one sighs and says, "Why, it will take many thousands to build chapels, and find ministers, and maintain missionaries," there is something hopeful in the calculation. All right, Philip, I am glad you have had your say and have shown the difficulty of the task. And then I like Andrew to get up and say, "It is a very difficult task, but still we must do what we can do, and as we have these five loaves and two small fish we must at least put these before the Lord, and leave it with him as to what is to be done."

All this is better than shirking the question altogether and leaving the crowd to starve.

Philip had his faculties exercised. Christ tested his arithmetic; he tested his eyesight; he tested his mind and spirit; and this prepared him to go and serve at the monster banquet which followed. A man never does a thing well till he has thought about it; and if Philip had not thought about how to feed the multitudes he would not have been a fit man to be employed in it. It prepared him also to adore his Master after the feast, for Philip would say when the meal was over, "The Master asked me how it was to be done, but I could not tell him, and now, though I have had a share in doing it, he must and shall have all the glory. He multiplied the fish, and increased the loaves. My poor faith can take no glory to itself. He did it. He did it all." Perhaps some question comes to you, my brother, about the Lord's work – "How can it be done? How can England be evangelized? How can the masses be reached? How can the world be made to hear the gospel?" Whatever the question is which is put to you, it is a question sent on purpose to do you good, and to benefit your soul, and to lead you to magnify the Lord all the more when the miracle of grace is done.

Now I come to the second part of the subject, and that is that there was no question with Jesus. The question was with Philip, but Christ had no question. *This He was saying to test him, for He Himself knew what He was intending to do.*

Let us take these words and pull them to pieces for a minute. *He Himself knew.* He always does know. "Ah," says one, "I am sure I do not know what I shall do." No, dear friend, and yet you have been taking advice, have you not? That is a splendid way of confusing yourself. I hear you cry in bewilderment, "I do not know. I have been to everybody, and I do not know what I shall do." That is a chronic state with us when we puzzle our own poor brains; but Jesus knew what he would do. This is sweet comfort; Jesus knows. He always knows all about it. He knew how many people there were. He knew how much bread it would take; he knew how many fish he would need, and how he meant to feed the crowd, and send them all away refreshed. He knew all before it happened.

Tested brother, Jesus knows all about *your* case and how he is going to bring you through. Do not think that you can inform him as to anything. *"For your Father knows what you need before you ask Him."* Prayer is not meant for the Lord's information. The question is not put to you so that you may instruct him, but that he may instruct you. He made the heavens and the earth without you. With whom did he take counsel? Who instructed him? And he will bring you through this present trial of yours without needing to add your poor wisdom to his infinite knowledge. He knows.

Jesus *knew what he would do.* He meant to do something, he was quite ready to do it, and he knew what he was going to do. We embarrass ourselves by saying, "Something must be done, but I do not know who is to do it." The Savior knew that something must be done, and he knew that he was going to do it himself. He was not in a hurry, he never is. "He never is before his time, he never is too late." Our blessed Master has glorious leisure because he is always punctual. Late people are in a hurry; but he, being never late, never hurries. He does everything calmly, because he foresees what he will do. Jesus knows, dear friend, concerning you, not only what you will do, but what he will do. That is the point, and he means to do some great thing for you and to help you. He means also to bring this city and this nation to his feet. He means that every knee shall bow to him, and that the whole earth shall be filled with his glory. He knows what he means to do.

> Prayer is not meant for the Lord's information.

He knew, moreover, *how he meant to do it.* He knew precisely the way and method which he intended to use. He perceived long before Andrew told him that there was a lad somewhere in the crowd with five barley loaves. When the lad set out that morning, I cannot make out what made him bring five barley loaves and fish into that crowd, except that the Master had whispered in his heart, "Young lad, take with you a good lunch. Put those barley loaves into the basket, and do not forget the fish. You do not know how long you may be from home." Nature bid him to provide for contingencies, but then nature is God's voice when he chooses to make it so. He was a hungry, growing lad with a fine appetite, and he meant to be well provided for; but had he ever thought in his mind that these strangely providential loaves would multiply so as to feed that mass of people? Where is the man that is to be the universal provider? Where is the chief of the commissariat? It is that youth, and that is the whole of his storehouse. He is carrying a stock of provisions on his back – in that basket.

The Savior knew that. And he knows exactly, dear friend, where your help is to come from in your hour of trouble. You do not know, but he does. He knows where the ministers are to come from that will stir up this city of London; and he knows in what style and manner they shall come, and how they shall get at the masses. When everybody else is defeated and in a quandary, he is fully prepared. He knew that those loaves and fish would be fetched out in due time to be the basis of a banquet; he knew that he would bless them, break them, multiply them, and give them to the disciples, and the disciples would give them to the multitude. Everything was arranged in his mind, and was as much fixed as the rising of the sun.

Once more, *he did it as one who knew what he was going to do.* How does a man act when he knows what he is going to do? Well, he generally proceeds in the most *natural* way. He knows that he is going to do it; so he just goes and does it. Can you conceive that a miracle was ever performed in a more natural style? If this had been a Roman Catholic miracle, they would have thrown the loaves up in the air, and they would have come down mysteriously transformed and multiplied a million times; all Catholic miracles, if you observe, have a great deal of the theatrical and showy about them. They are totally distinct from the miracles of Christ. He does this miracle in the most natural way in the world, because it is virtually the same miracle which Christ works every year. We take a certain quantity of wheat, and put it into the ground, and, in the long run, the end of it is that it is multiplied into loaves of bread. Certain fish are in the sea, and they increase into great shoals. The sown wheat passes through the same operation in the ground in the same hands – in God's hands, but it comes out as loaves of bread, and that is precisely what came of our Lord's action. He took a little into his own blessed hands, and broke it, and it kept on multiplying in his hands and in the hands of his disciples till they were all filled.

He knew what he was going to do, and so he did it naturally, and did it *orderly.* It is not so when a man does not know what he is to provide for. We have a large meeting, and there is provision made for tea, and three times as many come as you have provided for. What a hurry!

What a scurry! What a running to and fro! Jesus never conducts his matters in that way. He knew what he was going to do, and, therefore, he bid the men to sit down on the grass, and they sat down like so many children. Mark tells us that they sat down in *groups of hundreds and of fifties;* they were arranged as if each one had been specially set to his plate, and found his name laid upon it. Moreover, there was much grass in the place, so that the hall was carpeted in a way that no firm in London could have done it. The feast was conducted as orderly as if there had been notice given seven days beforehand and a contractor had supplied the provisions. Nothing could have been done in a better way, and it was all because Jesus knew what he would do.

Moreover, he did it very *joyfully.* He took bread and blessed it. He went about it with great pleasure. I would have liked to have seen his face as he looked on these poor famishing people being fed. Like a good host, he cheered them with his smile while he blessed them with the food.

And then he did it *plentifully,* for he knew what he would do; so he did not come half provided, or stint them so that every man should have only a little. No; he knew what he would do, and he measured their appetites exactly, a difficult thing when you have a number of hungry people to feed. He provided all that they wanted, and afterwards there was provision left for the head waiters, so that each one would have a basketful for himself; for they took up of the fragments twelve basketfuls – one for each of the headwaiters.

Our Lord Jesus Christ, in the matter of bringing in his own elect, is going about it, I am quite certain, knowing what he is going to do; and when you and I see the end of the great festival of mercy we shall say, "Blessed be the Lord! We were in a great worry; we were in sore trouble; but our Lord has done it easily and thoroughly. There has been no muddle, no crowding, no passing over of anybody. Blessed be his name! He has not done it by chance or through fortunate circumstances; but he knew what he would do, and he has planned it all through from the beginning to the end in such a way that principalities and powers in heaven shall sing forever of the grace and love and wisdom and power and care wherein he has abounded towards his people." Oh, but if we could see the end as well as the beginning we would begin even now to exalt the name of Jesus our Savior, who foreknows all his work, and never deviates from his plan.

I conclude by saying that because there is no question with Christ, though he puts questions to us, there ought to be no question of a doubtful character any longer to us. Let me mention three questions and I will be done.

The first question that troubles a great many people is, *How shall I bear my present burden?* How shall I endure this suffering? How shall I get a living? That question is sent to you to test you; but do remember that there is no question with Christ as to how you will get through, for *as thy days, so shall thy strength be*, and he will keep his saints, even to the end. Therefore, let there be no question with you, for Jesus himself knows what he will do. You came here today very distressed, and you said, "I wish I might get a word to tell me what I should do." You will not get half a word as to what *you* shall do, but you shall hear a word of a different sort. Jesus knows what he will do; and what he will do is infinitely better than anything you can do. Your strength, my friend, is to sit still. Roll your burden upon the Lord. Do the little you can do, and leave the rest with your heavenly Father. This is the answer from the Urim and the Thummim for you – Jesus knows what he will do.

There is that other question, which I have already brought up: *What is to be done with this great city?* I had the great privilege of being able to preach yesterday afternoon in one of our eastern suburbs, and setting out from my own house early in the morning, I went on riding, riding, upon one railway and another till I think I must have been journeying for fully two and a half hours before I had passed from one end of London to another. What a city of magnificent distances! It seems as if there was not a green tree which the builders will not cut down, nor a grassy meadow which they will not turn into ugly streets. "Replenish the earth," indeed? It is replenished. The dead earth is buried away beneath the abodes of living men. As for creatures of our race, what myriads there are of them!

And then, as you go along with a Christian friend, he says, "There is a chapel needed here," or "There is a little chapel here, but not one person in fifty goes to a place of worship." Then you arrive at another suburban place, and your guide will say, "Here are people anxious for the gospel, but there is nobody to take it to them." I went along yesterday sorely burdened and questioning in my heart, "What shall we do?" I kept thinking, "You had better not ask yourself that question, for you cannot do much towards answering it, and it will only worry you." And yet it came back to me, "How shall we buy bread for this multitude?" My Lord and Master would say *"we."* In my heart I wanted him to leave me out, but he would not. He never could have said, "How shall I buy bread?" because he knows that; but he put it to me, and I felt that I was a hindrance for making it a question at all, for he only makes it a question to me for my sake.

O that we had men and money to send out ministers and to build places for them to preach in. We have preachers ready in the college, but I have no means for building places of worship. Surely many of you must have been burdened with the hugeness of this city. But, dear, dear, this is like one drop of rain in a great shower compared with the whole world that lies in the hands of the wicked one. How is this world to be enlightened? It is no question with Jesus, and, therefore, it should never be an unbelieving question with us. "Can these dry bones live?" Let us answer, *"O Lord God, You know."* There will we leave it. He is able to do exceedingly abundantly above what we ask, or even think, and we may depend upon it that if he has sworn by himself that every knee shall bow, and every tongue confess to him, it shall be so, and he shall have the glory.

> He is able to do exceedingly abundantly above what we ask, or even think.

One other question should be mentioned. It is this: Has the Lord put into the heart of any unconverted person the question, *"What must I do to be saved?"* And is that question perplexing any of you? I am glad it is so, but I hope you will turn to the right place for an answer. I hope you are inquiring, "Lord, what would you have *me* to do?" Do you know why that question is put to you? It is to test you and to humble you. It is meant to make you feel the impossibility of salvation by your own works, so that you may submit yourself to the righteousness of God and be saved by faith in Christ Jesus.

Remember that there is no question with Christ about how you are to be saved. In fact, that question was settled – when? Shall I say?

Settled when he died? No, settled long before that. It was decided in the everlasting covenant before the morning star knew its place, or planets ran their round. God had then regarded his Son as the Lamb of God, slain before the foundation of the world, and to this day the word still stands – *"Behold, the Lamb of God, who takes away the sin of the world!"* Look unto him and be saved. There is no question about the possibility of your salvation, or about Christ's ability to save you. The question in your heart, "What must I do to be saved?" is put there to test you; but Jesus himself knows what he will do. What a blessed word is that! He knows how he will pardon, comfort, regenerate, instruct, and lead you. He knows how he will keep you to the end by his unchanging grace. He knows how he will preserve you, and sanctify you, and use you, and glorify his own name by you, and take you up to heaven, and set you upon his throne, and make all the angels wonder and adore, as they see what he will do. God bless you for Jesus' sake. Amen.

Chapter 9

The Boy's Loaves in the Lord's Hands

Jesus then took the loaves. (John 6:11)

Look, there are the people! Five thousand of them, as hungry as hunters, and they all need to have food given to them, for they cannot any of them travel to buy it! And here is the provision! Five thin wafers – and those of barley, more fit for horses than for men – and two little anchovies, by way of an appetizer! Five thousand people and five little biscuits by which to feed them! The disproportion is enormous: if each one should have only the tiniest crumb, there would not be enough. In like manner, there are millions of people in London, and only a handful of wholehearted Christians earnestly desiring to see the city converted to Christ. There are more than a thousand millions of men in this round world, and oh, so few missionaries breaking to them the Bread of Life, almost as few for the millions as were these five barley loaves for those five thousand! The problem is a very difficult one. The contrast between the supply and the demand would have struck us much more vividly if we had been there, in that crowd at Bethsaida, than it does sitting here, nearly nineteen hundred years afterwards, and merely hearing about it. But the Lord Jesus was equal to the emergency; none of the people went away without sharing in his bounty; they were all filled.

Our blessed Master, now that he has ascended into the heavens, has more power rather than less power. He is not baffled because of our lack, but can even now use inferior means to accomplish his own glorious purposes; therefore, let no man's heart fail him. Do not despair of the evangelization of London, nor think it hopeless that the gospel should be preached in all nations for a testimony unto them. Have faith in God, who is in Christ Jesus; have faith in the compassion of the Great Mediator. He will not desert the people in their spiritual need, any more than he failed that hungry throng in their worldly need long ago.

We will now look at these biscuits and sardines, which seem to be truly an insufficient stock-in-trade to begin with, a very small amount indeed on which to conduct the business of feeding five thousand persons. I shall say of these loaves and fish, first, that *they had a previous history* before being mentioned in our text; secondly, when we get to our text, we shall find these little things *in a very grand position – Jesus then took the loaves;* and therefore, thirdly, *they will have an after-history* which is well worthy of being noted. When things get into Christ's hands, they are in the very focus of miracles.

We will begin by saying that these loaves and fish had a previous history. Andrew said to Jesus, *"There is a lad here who has five barley loaves and two fish."*

Notice first, then, *the providence of God in bringing the lad there.* We do not know his name; we are not told anything concerning his parentage. Was he a little peddler who thought that he could make some money by selling a few loaves and fish, and had he nearly sold out? Or was he a boy that the apostles had employed to carry this meager provision for the use of Jesus and his friends? We do not know much about him, but he was the right boy in the right place that day. Whatever his name might be, it did not matter; he had the barley loaves and fish upon which the people were to be fed. Christ never is in need but that he has somebody at hand to supply that need. Have faith in the providence of God. What made the boy bring the loaves and fish, I do not know. Boys often do unaccountable things; but bring the loaves and fish he did, and God, who understands the ideas and motives of lads, and takes account even of barley loaves and fish, had appointed that boy to be there. Again I say, believe in the providence of God.

Mr. Stanley tells us that when he came out of that long journey of his through the forest, I think after 160 days of walking in darkness, and found himself at last where he could see the sun, he felt that there was a special providence of God that had taken care of him. I am very glad that Mr. Stanley felt that it was the hand of God that had brought him out of the unhealthy shade; but I do not need to go to Africa to learn that we are surrounded behind and before by his goodness. Many of us have felt a special providence of God in our own bedrooms; we have met with his hand in connection with our own children. Yes, every day we are surrounded by tokens of his care. *Who is wise? Let him give heed to these things, and consider the lovingkindness of the Lord.* "I am sure God took care of me," said one, "for as I was going along a certain street, I slipped on a piece of orange peel, and had what might have been a serious fall; yet I was not hurt in the least." To this his friend replied, "I am sure God has taken care of *me;* for I have walked along that street hundreds of times, and have never slipped on a piece of orange peel, or on anything else." Very often God draws near to us in common life.

> He comes to us all unaware,
> And makes us own his loving care.

Let us also believe in his providence with regard to the church of Christ: he will never desert his people; he will find men when he wants them. Thus it has ever been in the history of the saints, and thus it shall ever be. Before the Reformation there were many learned men who knew something of Christ's gospel, but they said that it was a pity to make a noise, and so they communed with one another and with Christ very quietly. What was needed was some rough, bullheaded fellow who would blurt the gospel out and upset the old state of things. Where could he be found?

There was a monk named Luther, who, while he was reading his Bible, suddenly stumbled on the doctrine of justification by faith; he was the man. Yet when he went to a dear brother in the Lord and told him how he felt, his friend said to him, "Go back to your cell, and pray and commune with God, and hold your tongue." But then, you see, he had a tongue that he could not hold, and that nobody else could hold, and he began to speak with it the truth that had made a new man of him. The God that made Luther, knew what he was at when he made him; he put within him a great burning fire that could not be restrained, and it burst forth and set the nations on a blaze. Never despair about providence. There sits today, somewhere in a chimney corner in the country, a man that will turn the current of unbelief, and win back the churches to the old gospel. God never yet did come to a point of distress as to his truth but what suddenly one came forward, a David with a sling and a stone, or a Samson with a jawbone, or a Shamgar with an oxgoad, who put to rout the adversaries of the Lord. *"There is a lad here."* The providence of God had sent him.

Next, *this lad with his loaves was brought into notice.* When they were searching for all the provisions in the company, this obscure boy, that never would have been heard of otherwise, was brought to the front because he had his little basket of biscuits. Andrew found him out, and he came and said to Jesus, *"There is a lad here who has five barley loaves and two fish."* So, rest assured, that if you have the Bread of Life around you, and you are willing to serve God, you need not be afraid that obscurity will ever prevent your doing it. "Nobody knows me," says one. Well, it is not a very desirable thing that anybody should know you; those of us who are known to everybody would be very glad if we were not; there is no very great comfort in it. He that can work away for his Master, with nobody to see him but his Master, is the happiest of men.

"I have only one hundred people to preach to," said a country pastor to me; and I replied, "If you give a good account of those hundred, you have quite enough to do." If all you have is very little – just that pennyworth of loaves and fish – use that properly, and you will do your Master service; and in due time, when God wants you, he knows where to find you. You need not put an advertisement in the paper; he knows the street you live on, and the number on the door. You need not go and push yourself to the front; the Lord will bring you to the front when he wants you, and I hope that you do not want to get there if he does not want you to. Depend upon it, should you push forward when you are not required, he will put you back again. Oh, for grace to work on unobserved, to have your one talent, your five loaves and two fish, and only to be noticed when the hour suggests the need, and the need makes a loud call for you. We have thus seen, first of all, the loaves and fish, in the desert, quite unnoticed, but put there by Providence; and we now behold them by that same Providence, thrust into prominence.

When brought into notice, the loaves and fish did not fare very well; *they were judged insufficient for the purpose;* for Andrew said, *"What are these for so many people?"* The boy's candle seemed to be quite snuffed out: so small a stock – what could be the use of that? Now, I dare say that some of you have had Satan saying to you, "What is the use of your trying to do anything?" To you, dear mother, with a family of children, he has whispered, "You cannot serve God." He knows very well that, by sustaining grace, you can; and he is afraid of how well you can serve God if you bring up those dear children in reverence of him. He says to the seller of religious books over yonder, "You have not much ability; what can you do?"

Ah, dear friend! he is afraid of what you can do, and if you will only do what you can do, God will, by and by, help you to do what now you cannot do. But the devil is afraid of even the little that you can do now; and many a child of God seems to side with Satan in despising the day of small things. *"What are these for so many people?"* So few, so poor, so devoid of talent, what can any of us hope to do? Scorned, even by the disciples, it is small wonder if we are held in contempt by the world. The things that God will honor, man must first despise. You run the gauntlet of the derision of men, and afterwards you come out to be used of God.

Though seemingly inadequate to feed the multitude, these loaves and fish would have been quite enough for the boy's supper, yet *he appears to have been quite willing to part with them.* The disciples would not have taken them from him by force; the Master would not have allowed it. The lad willingly gave them up to be the beginning of the great feast. Somebody might have said, "John, you know that you will soon be able to eat those five loaves and those two little fish; keep them; get away into a corner: every man for himself." Is it not a good rule, "Take care of number one"? Yes, but the boy whom God uses will not be selfish. Am I speaking to some young Christian to whom Satan says, "Make money first, and serve God by and by. Stick to business, and get on; then, after that, you can act like a Christian, and give some money away," and so on? Let such a one remember the barley loaves and the fish.

If that lad had really wisely studied his own interests instead of merely yielding with a generous impulse to the demand of Christ, he would have done exactly what he did; for if he had kept the loaves, he would have eaten them, and there would have been an end of them; but now that he brings them to Christ, all those thousands of people are fed, and he gets as much himself as he would have had if he had eaten his own stock. And then, in addition, he gets a share out of the twelve baskets full of fragments that remain. Anything that you take away from self and give to Christ is well invested; it will often bring in ten thousand percent. The Lord knows how to give such a reward to an unselfish man, so that he will feel that he who saves his life loses it, but he who is willing even to lose his life, and the bread that sustains it, is the man who, after all, gets truly saved.

This, then, is the history of these loaves. They were sent there through God's providence by a lad who was sought out and brought into notice. His stock-in-trade was despised, but he was willing to give it, whether it was despised or not. He would yield it to his Lord. Now, do you see what I am driving at? I want to get ahold of some of the lads, and some young men and young women – I will not be troubled about your age; you shall be lads if you are under seventy – I want to get ahold of you who think that you have very little ability, and say to you, "Come, and bring it to Jesus." We want you. Times are hard. The people are famishing. Though nobody seems to need you, yet be bold to come out; and who knows but that, like Queen Esther, you may have come to the kingdom for such a time as this? God may have brought you where you are to make use of you for the converting of thousands; but you must be converted yourself first. Christ will not use you unless you are first his own. You must yield yourself up to him, and be saved by his precious blood, and then, after that, come and yield up to him all the little talent that you may have, and pray him to make as much use of you as he did of the lad with the five barley loaves.

But now I want to show you that these barley loaves got into a grand position. The text says, *Jesus then took the loaves*. He took them into his own hands. From the trembling hands of the boy, or from his little basket, they were transferred to the blessed hands which one day would bear the nail-prints. This may teach us several lessons.

First, *they were now associated with Jesus Christ.* From this point on, those loaves do not so much suggest the thought of the lad's sacrifice as of the Savior's power. Is it not a wonderful thing that Christ, the living God, should associate himself with our feebleness, with our lack of talent, with our ignorance, with our little faith? And yet he does so. If we are not associated with him, we can do nothing; but when we come into living touch with him, we can do all things. Those barley loaves in Christ's hands become pregnant with food for all the crowd. Out of his hands they are nothing but barley loaves; but in his hands, associated with him, they are in contact with omnipotence. Have you who love the Lord Jesus Christ thought of this, of bringing all that you possess to him so that it may be associated with him?

There is that brain of yours; it can be associated with the teachings of his Spirit. There is that heart of yours; it can be warmed with the love of God. There is that tongue of yours; it can be touched with the live coal from off the altar. There is that manhood of yours; it can be perfectly consecrated by association with Christ. Hear the tender command of the Lord: *"Bring them here to Me,"* and your whole life will be transformed. I do not say that every man of common ability can rise to high ability by being associated with Christ through faith; but I do say this – that his ordinary ability, in association with Christ, will become sufficient for the occasion to which God in providence has called him. I know that you have been praying, and saying, "I do not have this, and I cannot do that." Do not stop to number your deficiencies; bring what you have, and let all that you are – body, soul, and spirit – be associated with Christ. Although he will not bestow upon you new functions, the functions you have will have new power, for they will come into a new condition towards him, and what may not be hoped for by association with such wisdom and might?

But, further, *they were transferred to Christ.* A moment ago they belonged to this lad, but now they belong to Christ. *Jesus then took the loaves.* He has taken possession of them; they are his property. Oh, Christian people, do you mean what you say when you declare that you have given yourselves to Christ? If you have made a full transfer, therein will lie great power for usefulness. But do not people often say, "If I might make some reserve"? *"What then is this bleating of the sheep in my ears, and the lowing of the oxen which I hear?"* What about that odd thousand that you put in the funds the other day? What about the money saved up for a new bonnet? You sometimes sing –

> Yet if I might make some reserve,
>   And duty did not call,
> I love my God with zeal so great,
>   That I should give him all.

Ah, well! when you have really yielded all, you may sing that again, but I am afraid that there are but few who can sing it truly. Oh, that we had more real putting of the loaves into Christ's hands! The time that you have not used for self, but have given to Christ; the knowledge that you have not stored, as in a reservoir, but have given to Christ; the ability that you have not wielded for the world, but have yielded to Christ; your influence and position, your money and home, all put into Christ's hands, and reckoned to be not your own, but to be his from this point on – this is the way in which London's need will be met, and the world's hunger will be satisfied. But we are astonished at the very outset by the lack of this complete dedication of everything to Christ.

What is better still, as these loaves were given to Jesus, so *they were accepted by Jesus.* They were not only dedicated, they were also consecrated. Jesus took the five barley loaves, Jesus took the two little fish, and in doing so he seemed to say, "These will do for me." As the American Standard Version has it, *Jesus **therefore** took the loaves* (emphasis added). Was there any reason why he should? Yes, because they were brought to him; they were willingly presented to him; there was a need of them, and he could work with them. *Therefore* he took the loaves. Children of God, if Christ has ever made use of you, you have often stood and wondered how the Lord could ever accept you; but there was a "therefore" in it. He saw that you were willing to win souls. He saw that the souls needed winning, and he used you, even *you.* Am I not now speaking to some who might be of great service if they yielded themselves unto Christ, and Christ accepted them, and they became accepted in the beloved? Only five barley loaves, but Jesus accepted them; only two small fish, brought by a little lad, but the great Christ accepted them, and they became his own. Let us join one now in heaven, who on earth brought her all, and pray –

> Oh, use me, Lord, use even me,
> Just as thou wilt, and when, and where:
> Until thy blessed face I see,
> Thy rest, thy joy, thy glory share!

But, what is better still, *these loaves and fish were blessed by Christ* as he lifted up his eyes and gave thanks to the Father for them. Think of it. For five little loaves and two little fish Christ gave thanks to the Father, apparently a meager cause for praise, but Jesus knew what he could make of them, and therefore he gave thanks for what they would presently accomplish. "God loves us," says Augustine, "for what we are becoming." Christ gave thanks for these trifles because he saw to what end they would grow. Do you not think that having thanked the Father, he also thanked the boy? And in later years these words of gratitude would be ample recompense for such a tiny deed.

Like the woman who cast in the two mites to the treasury, he gave his all, and doubtless was commended for the gift. Though high in glory today, Christ is still grateful when such offerings are made to him; still he thanks his Father when, with timid, trembling hands, we offer to him our best, our all, however small. Still is his heart gladdened when we bring him our meager store that it may be touched by his dear hand, and blessed by his gracious lips. He loves us not for what we are, but for what he will yet make us; he blesses our offerings not for their worth, but because his power will yet make them worthy of his praise. May the Lord thus bless every talent that you have! May he bless your memory; may he bless your understanding; may he bless your voices; may he bless your hearts; may he bless your heads; may he bless you all and evermore! When he puts a blessing into

> He blesses our offerings not for their worth, but because his power will yet make them worthy of his praise.

the little gift and into the little grace that we have, good work begins, and goes on to perfection.

And when the loaves had been blessed, the next thing was, *they were increased by Christ.* Peter takes one, begins to break it, and as he breaks it, he has always as much in his hand as he started with. "Here, take a bit of fish, friend," says he. He gives a whole fish to that man; he has a whole fish left. So he gives it to another, and another, and another, and goes on scattering the bread and scattering the fish everywhere, as quickly as he can; and when he is done, he has his hands just as full of fish and as full of bread as ever. If you serve God you will never run dry. He who gives you something to say one Sunday will give you something to say another Sunday.

These seven-and-thirty years and more, I have ministered to this same church and congregation, and every time that I have preached I have said all that I knew. Some very learned brethren are like the great barrel of Heidelberg; they can hold so much wine that there is enough to swim in, but they put in a tap somewhere up at the top, and you never get much out. Mine is a very small barrel indeed, but the tap is down as low as it can be; and you can get more wine out of a small tub, if you empty it, than you can out of a big vat if you are only permitted to draw a little from the top. This boy gave all his loaves, and all his fish – not much, truly – but Christ multiplied it. Be like him, give your all; do not think of reserving some for another occasion. If you are a preacher, do not think of what you will preach about the next time; think of what you are going to preach about now. It is always quite enough to get one sermon at a time; you need not have a store, because if you get a lot piled away somewhere, there will be a stale odor about them. Even the manna that came down from heaven bred worms and stunk; so will your best sermons, even if the message is God-given; and if it does not come down from heaven, but from your own brain, it will go bad still more quickly.

Tell the people about Christ. Lead them to Jesus, and do not be troubled about what you will say next time, but wait till next time comes, and it shall be given you in the same hour what you shall speak.

But, mark once more: when Jesus took the loaves, it was not only to multiply, but also to distribute them. *They were distributed by Christ.*

He did not believe in multiplication, unless it was accompanied by division. Christ's additions mean subtraction, and Christ's subtractions mean additions. He gives that we may give away. He multiplied as soon as the disciples began to distribute; and when the distribution ended, the multiplication ended. Oh, for grace to go on distributing! If you have received the truth from Christ, tell it out! God will whisper it in your ear, and tell it in; but if you stop the telling out, if you cease the endeavor to bless others, it may be that God will no more bless you, nor grant you again the communion of his face.

Putting all this together, if we all would bring our loaves and fish to the Lord Jesus Christ, he would take them and make them wholly his own. Then, when he would have blessed them, he would multiply them, and he would bid us to distribute them, and we could yet meet the needs of London, and the needs of the whole world even to the last man. A Christ who could feed five thousand can feed five million. There is no limit. When once you get a miracle, you may as well have a great one. Whenever I find the critics paring down miracles, it always seems to me to be very poor work; for if it is a miracle, it is a miracle; and if you are in for a penny, you may as well be in for a pound. If you can believe that Christ can feed fifty, then you can believe that he can feed five hundred, five thousand, five million, or five hundred million, if it pleases him.

> A Christ who could feed five thousand can feed five million. There is no limit.

Thus have I tried to stir up God's people to believe in the Lord and consecrate themselves to him. But some of you are saying, "He is not preaching to me." No, I am not preaching *to* you, but I am preaching *for* you; for if God's people begin to be roused, they will soon look after you. You will have somebody asking you about your soul before you get out of the tabernacle; and during the week, if you meet some of them, they will be troubling you, rousing up your conscience, and making you feel what an awful thing it is to be an enemy to God, and to live without Christ. I hope that it will be so. Oh, you who do not love my Lord, what are you at? Paul said that you would be *Anathema Maranatha* – cursed at his coming! I pray you, do not rest easy while that may be your portion. You are the people that we want to feed; you are the people whom we want to bless. Oh, that God in his mercy would but bless you! We do not ask to have the honor of it. We would be willing to have it quite unknown who it was that brought you to the Savior, so long as you did but come to him. May the Lord in mercy bring you!

But now, thirdly, and to conclude, these loaves and fish had an after-history. They got into Christ's hands. What was the result?

First, *a great deal of misery was removed* by the lad's basketful of barley loaves. Those poor people were famished; they had been with Christ all day, and had had nothing to eat; and had they been dispersed as they were, tired and hungry, many of them would have fainted by the way; perhaps some would even have died. Oh, what would we give if we might but alleviate the misery of this world! I remember the Earl of Shaftesbury saying, "I should like to live longer. I cannot bear to go out of the world while there is so much misery in it." And you know how that dear saint of God laid himself out to look after the poor, and the helpless, and the needy all his days. Perhaps I speak to some who have not woken up yet to the idea that if they were to bring their little all to Christ, he could make use of it in alleviating the misery of many a wounded conscience, and that awful misery which will come upon men if they die unforgiven and stand before the judgment bar of God without a Savior. Yes, young man, God can make you the spiritual father of many.

As I look back upon my own history, little did I dream when first I opened my mouth for Christ, in a very humble way, that I should have the honor of bringing thousands to Jesus. Blessed, blessed be his name! He gets the glory for it. But I cannot help thinking that there must be some other lad here, such a one as I was, whom he may call by his grace to do service for him. When I had a letter sent to me by the deacons of the church at New Park Street to come up to London to preach, I sent it back by the next post, telling them that they had made a mistake, that I was a lad of nineteen years of age, happy among a very poor and lowly people in Cambridgeshire who loved me, and that I did not imagine that they could mean that I was to preach in London. But they returned it to me and said that they knew all about it, and I must come.

Ah, what a story it has been since then, of the goodness and loving-kindness of the Lord! Now, perhaps, these words come to some brother who has never yet laid hold of the idea that God can use him. You must not think that God picks out all the very choice and particularly fine persons. It is not so in the Bible; some of those that he took were very rough people: even the first apostles were mostly fishermen. Paul was an educated man, but he was like a lot out of the catalog, one born out of due time. The rest of them were not so, but God used them; and it still pleases God, by *the base things* and *the things that are not, so that He may nullify the things that are.* I do not want you to think highly of yourself; your loaves are only five, and they are barley, and poor barley at that; and your fish are very small, and there are only two of them. I do not want you to think much of them, but think much of Christ, and believe that, whoever you may be, if he thought it worth his while to buy you with his blood, and is willing to make some use of you, it is surely worth your while to come and bring yourself, and all that you have, to him who is thus graciously ready to accept you. Put everything into his hands, and let it be said of you today, *Jesus then took the loaves.* It is a part of the history of the loaves that they assuaged a great mass of misery.

And next, *Jesus was glorified;* for the people said, *"This is truly the Prophet who is to come into the world."* The miracle of the loaves carried them back to the wilderness, and to the miracle of the manna. They remembered that Moses had said, *"God will raise up for you a prophet like me from your brethren."* For this Deliverer they longed, and as the bread increased so grew their wonder, until in the swelling loaves they saw the finger of God, and said, *"This is truly the Prophet who is to come into the world."* That little lad became, by his loaves and fish, the revealer of Christ to all the multitude; and who can tell, if you give your loaves to Christ, whether thousands may not recognize him as the Savior because of it? Christ is still known in the breaking of bread. But the people went further with reference to Christ, after they had been fed by the loaves and fish: they concluded that he was a prophet, and they began whispering among themselves, "Let us make him a king." Now, in a better sense than the text implies, I wish to God that you and I, though humbly and feebly, might serve Christ till people said, "Christ is a prophet. Let us make him a king." This sermon I offer my Master, if he will be pleased to accept it, though it is but a barley loaf, and I pray that by it some may take Jesus Christ to be their king. Oh, that he had a throne in the hearts of many whom he shall feed at this time with the bread of heaven!

Brethren, I know that you wish to glorify Christ. Here is the way. Bring your loaves and fish to Christ so that he may use them in his divine commissariat, and then he shall be magnified in the eyes of all the people.

When the feast was finished, *there were fragments to be gathered.* This is a part of the history of the loaves – they were not lost; they were eaten, but they were there; people were filled with them, but yet there was more of them left than when the feast began. Each disciple had a basketful to carry back to his Master's feet. Give yourself to Christ, and when you have used yourself for his glory, you will be more able to serve him than you are now; you shall find your little stock grow as you spend it. Remember Bunyan's picture of the man who had a roll of cloth. He unrolled it, and he cut off so much for the poor. Then he unrolled it, and cut off some more, and the more he cut it, the longer it grew. Upon which Bunyan remarks –

> There was a man, and some did count him mad;
> The more he gave away, the more he had.

It is certainly so with talent and ability, and with grace in the heart. The more you use it, the more there is of it. It is often so with gold and silver: the store of the liberal man increases, while the miser grows poor. We have an old proverb, which is as true as it is suggestive: "Drawn wells have the sweetest waters." So, if you keep continually drawing on your mind, your thoughts will get sweeter; and if you continue to draw on your strength, your strength will get to be more mighty through God. The more you do, the more you may do, by the grace of the ever-blessed One!

The more you do, the more you may do, by the grace of the ever-blessed One!

Last of all, it came to pass, that *these loaves had a record made about them.* There is many a loaf that has gone to a king's table and yet has never been chronicled; but this boy's five loaves and two little fish have gotten into the Bible. If you look, you will find the barley loaves in Matthew; you will find the barley loaves in Mark; you will find the barley loaves in Luke, you will find the barley loaves, where we have found our text, in John. To make quite sure that we should never forget how much God can do with little things, this story is told four times over, and it is the only one of Christ's miracles which has such an abundant record.

And now, as a practical issue, let us put it to the test. You young people who have lately joined the church, do not let it be long before you try to do something for Christ. You who have for a long time been trusting Christ, and have never yet begun to work, arouse yourselves to attempt some service for his sake. Aged friends and sick friends can still find something to do. Perhaps, at the last, it will be found that the persons whom we might have excused on account of illness, or weakness, or poverty are the people who have done the most. That, at least, is my observation. I find that, if there is a really good work done, it is usually done by an invalid, or by somebody who might very properly have said, "I pray you, have me excused." How is it that so many able-bodied and gifted Christians seem to be so slow in the Master's service? If there is a political meeting, something about liberals and conservatives, how earnest you are! You are all there, every bit of you, over your politics, which are not worth a penny a year; but when it comes to souls being saved, many of you are as mute as fish. You go all the year round without caring even for the spiritual welfare of a little child.

One of our friends gave a good answer to a brother who said to him, "I have been a member of a church now for forty years. I am a father in Israel." He asked him, "How many children have you? How many have you brought to Christ?" "Well," the man said, "I do not know that I ever brought anybody to Christ," upon which our friend retorted, "Call yourself a father in Israel, and yet you have no children! I think you had better wait until you have earned the title." So do I. It would be better that we had no persons who profess such, but that all our members, even if there were fewer of them, should be men and women constantly bringing forth fruit unto God in the conversion of others. The Lord set you all to work with this object!

I am almost done; but again I cannot help reminding those who are not Christ's, that while I have not directly preached to them, I have tried, by a side wind, to be preaching to them all the time. Either you are the Lord's, or you are not. If you are Christ's servant, take a sheet of paper and write down, "Lord, I bring my loaves and fish to you"; and if you are not Christ's, confess the awful truth to yourself and face it. I wish that you would make a record of it in black and white, putting down both name and date: *"I am not Christ's."* Take a good look at it, try and grasp what it means to withhold yourself from him who loves you and waits to save; then ask yourself why you are not his.

I remember a woman, not long ago, who said that at her work it came across her mind, "I am not saved." She was sweeping the room, and when she finished that, she said to herself, "I have to cook the dinner, but I am not saved." She went into the kitchen, and had her fire all ready, and her food; but while she was putting things in the pot she kept saying to herself, "I am not saved"; and so it was while she was busy all the afternoon. When her husband came home, she could not help blurting it out to him, "Oh, husband, I am not saved!" But he was, and he pointed her to Christ. They knelt together, and oh, how he prayed with her! She found that which she so earnestly sought, and it was not very many days before she could say, "Oh, husband, I am saved!" May that be the case with you! The Lord bless every one of you, wherever you may be! We shall all meet in the day of judgment. May you and I meet without fear there, to sing to the sovereign grace of God, which saved us from the wrath to come, and helped us while we were here to bring our little, and put it into Christ's hands! The Lord be with you! Amen.

Chapter 10

The Miracle of the Loaves

They had not gained any insight from the incident of the loaves. (Mark 6:52)

Let us with deep attention consider the miracle of the loaves, lest we fall into the same evil as that which happened to the disciples in the text. When they saw Jesus walking on the sea *they were utterly astonished, for they had not gained any insight from the incident of the loaves, but their heart was hardened.* Hard hearts and painful unbelief spring up in the waste places where we bury our forgotten mercies. The miracles of our Lord Jesus Christ ought to be considered; they are not trifles, and they ought not to be passed over as if they were the mere commonplaces of a daily newspaper. Everything that has to do with the Son of God is a suitable subject for the deepest study, and all his sayings and doings should be sought out by them that have pleasure therein. Neither earth nor heaven, neither time nor eternity yields choicer gems of thought than the achievements of our Lord.

Remember, that since Jesus Christ is the same yesterday, today, and forever, what he did at one time ought to be well considered, because it is the index of what he is prepared to do again should the need arise. Still would he sooner feed his own sheep by a miracle than allow them to lack any good thing. His accomplished wonders have not used up his strength; he has the dew of his youth still upon him. Our Samson's locks are not shaved; our Solomon has not lost his wisdom; our Immanuel has not ceased to be "God with us."

If the disciples had considered the miracle of the loaves they would have observed that Christ is grand at emergencies. When there were five thousand people to be fed and no towns and villages near enough to supply them with bread, so that the people would faint by the way before they could reach the markets, then Christ was ready, full-handed in time of scarcity, prompt to dispense his liberality, and able to meet the emergency so perfectly that the people must have been very thankful that such an emergency had arisen, and no doubt often wished that they could have been in such distress again if they could have had the Lord near to bring them out of it. Had they considered the miracle of the loaves, the disciples would have known that Christ not only is grand at emergencies, but that he also displays his power spontaneously, without need of pressing or even prompting. Before anybody else had cared for the multitude he began inquiring about the state of the stores from which the famishing ones must be fed. He it was who thought of the way of feeding them; it was a design invented and originated by himself. His followers had looked at their little store of bread and fish and given up the task as hopeless; but Jesus, altogether unembarrassed, and in no perplexity, had already considered how he would banquet the thousands and make the fainting sing for joy. The Lord of Hosts needed no pleading to become the host of hosts of hungry men.

Remembering this, the disciples in their new distress should have said within themselves, "Now will he display his power. We scarcely have any need to cry to him, because before we call he will answer, and while the emergency is yet pressing upon our minds he will hear." But they forgot what he had done on that occasion, and therefore they fell into distrust as to their new trial. Beloved, is not this a very common fault with us? Do we not too often forget what the Lord has done for us in times past? We sing so rightly –

> His love in time past forbids me to think
> He'll leave me at last in trouble to sink;
> Each sweet Ebenezer I have in review
> Confirms his good pleasure to help me quite through.

But do we not forget those Ebenezers? Do we not very frequently permit our memory to let his benefits go? Is not depression of spirit occasioned by the fact that we do not well consider the miracle of the loaves or its counterpart which has taken place in our history? How many times have I sought the Lord in sorest trouble and he has brought me through! What burdens have I carried to him and found them vanish! What needs has he not supplied? What marvels has he not worked on my behalf? Surely, if I think of what he has done for me I shall not, unless my heart be hardened, permit myself to be afraid. Cannot many of you say the same? Are there not oases in your pilgrimage through the desert which, as you look back upon them, are to your grateful memory very green and full of sunlight, where the Lord revealed himself to you and worked very mightily for you? Consider, then, the miracle of the loaves as it has transpired in your own life story, and be not afraid, whatever your present trouble may be.

At the present time I shall not consider the miracle of the loaves in the form of a sermon, but I will allow our discourse to take the shape of a little friendly talk.

Come, let us think a little, first, about the guests who gathered around our Lord when he worked the miracle of the loaves.

And we are struck, first, with *their great number*. Jesus had his feast days, when he kept open house and entertained his guests in unusual crowds. Twice, especially, he held very remarkable feasts, and his banquets were distinguished for the number that came to them. Here were five thousand men, and on another occasion some four thousand men, besides women and children, and I should think that is a very large "besides," for the women and children may possibly have outnumbered the men; at least, they often do so in our congregations nowadays. This was feasting on an imperial scale. In the present instance five thousand gathered together, and all were as easily provided for as if there had been only five.

Should we not consider this point, and argue from it that the Lord Jesus will feed our hungry souls if we come to him? Should we not each one say, then, If I am a soul wanting his love and mercy, surely he can bless me? Are there a great many saved already? Are hundreds pressing to the Savior at this very hour? Then why should I be shut out? He who could feed five thousand could certainly feed five thousand and one. One more or less could make no difference at so great a feast. No, I am quite certain Jesus can supply me, for he had twelve baskets left after he had fed all the host. Come, my soul, if you are hungering after Christ, do not stand back as though you would be one too many. The more the merrier. The more that come to his gospel banquet the more pleased Jesus is. Some religionists are in raptures with the text: *"For the gate is small and the way is narrow that leads to life, and there are few who find it"*; and they dwell upon the words *"there are few who find it"* with an evident gusto and self-appreciation, something like the old conservative voter when he denounced household suffrage, and gloried in his own monopoly.

Such thoughts are not according to the mind of Christ. He did not say, "I will feed five hundred of these people, and the rest may starve"; but in the mighty generosity of his heart, the greatness of their number, and the direness of their need, moved him to come forward and supply them all. Had there been fifty, they might have gone home as on other occasions, for fifty might possibly have found food in the villages; but the needs of five thousand required a divine supply. The greatness of the number of sinners seems both to encourage our Lord to act in mercy, and to make it divinely suitable that he should act; for by his knowledge shall he justify *many*, and bring *many* sons unto glory. Let no sinner ever be troubled with the dread that he would be one too many at the banquet of mercy, neither let him fear that he will be an intruder. Christ's banqueting hall was an open field; there were no walls or doors, or persons guarding the entrance; thus free is his feast of love at this moment. Whosoever will, let him come.

We note next *the strange character of his guests*. We do not know what sort of people they were, but this we do know: he did not exempt one because of any specialty in his character. They were a dull multitude. Little good could be said of them, except that they had an ear to hear Jesus preach, and were especially glad if the sermon was the first course, with loaves and fish for the second. They were a carnal people, and had nothing about them that deserved our Lord's consideration. But when did Jesus Christ wait until men deserved it before he blessed them? When we give charity, we think it fitting to make inquiries about the deserving characters of those who appeal to us for relief, and I suppose we must do so, or we shall do mischief. But our heavenly Father sends his rain both upon the just and upon the unjust, and even so our Lord Jesus Christ feeds these people, though many of them were mere loafers and hangers-on. Bad or good, the generous Savior fed them. It could not hurt them to have a bit of bread and fish to eat, for a gift of food which people eat before our eyes is generally safe charity, and so the Master fed them.

Let me, then, say to myself, I may be very unworthy, and I am, and my character may have nothing about it to commend it to the Lord Jesus Christ; but why should he not feed me with the food that is necessary for my soul? Has he not come into the world to save sinners? Did he not visit this world as a physician to heal the sick? Let not my unworthiness keep me back. Lack of merit did not exclude one person from the miracle of the loaves, and it need not exclude me, for he bids me to come. I unworthy as I am, he invites me freely, repeatedly, earnestly; yes, he commands me to come. Why, then, should I hesitate? If there be many, I will be one among them; and if they be of all kinds, I may the more freely join them.

These guests had one thing in common, which I have no doubt will be found among us also – *they were all hungry, and they were all poor.* They could not supply one single dish for the table. Not one of them had a loaf to contribute nor a fish to give to the Master of the feast. They were all hungry, but not one could produce a crust; and the Lord neither asked them to contribute nor repelled them because of their poverty. Am I, then, today, an empty sinner, having no good in myself? Do I feel that I could not contribute even one perfect thought, much less one solitary perfect action to the stores of the Redeemer's merit? Nevertheless, he bids me to come, and come I will. He is a great giver; I can only be a receiver, and my utter lack of all goodness suits me to receive from him, since the emptier the vessel the more it can receive. If I could help him there would be no need for him to work a miracle on my account, but since I can bring nothing whatsoever, I need his miraculous power. As I see him feeding hungry souls I will join in with the rest and partake of the fruit of his compassion. They were a penniless, foodless people, and they could not help themselves; but there was one who could help them all, and bestow that help with ease. And so, today, whatever our hearts' necessities may be, Jesus is here to enrich us, and to do it in a manner which will manifest the boundless nature of his love and grace.

On one of these occasions we read that *there were women and children among them.* Now, I must confess myself I am not partial to very small children coming into the congregation. I am glad to see their mothers, and if they cannot come without bringing their infants, I am glad that they should bring them; but they certainly are not an improvement to a congregation, as a rule. Yet here they were; here were women and children, and I suppose that some of the children were very closely connected with the women by being carried in their arms, because they are described as *women **and children*** (emphasis added). They were all fed, and that would stop their crying; they were all supplied, however little they might be.

And should not this be a great encouragement to me if I am seeking Christ, that if I be no better than a little crying child that might seem to be a nuisance in God's family, or if I be a person so poor, so unacceptably clothed, that I may seem to myself to be as much out of place in a congregation as a crying babe, yet, nevertheless, the bounties of divine grace are as much for me as for others? Jesus would not have it said that he had no food for the children. He would not have the mothers go home and say, "The big men had their food, but we had only a few bones and broken scraps, and the poor dear children had none at all." In Christ's feasts there is no complaining of the widows as in apostolic days. None are neglected in the general ministration when Jesus presides; but whosoever will, may come and partake of the bounties which the King of heaven has prepared for every hungry, thirsty soul.

So much about the guests. May those suggestions be blessed by the Holy Spirit to induce some hungry sinner to join with the rest of the company, and feast on free grace.

The next thing we will consider in the miracle of the loaves is the orderliness of the guests. There were five thousand, but *they sat down in groups of hundreds and of fifties.* I wonder how they were marshalled so well? Oh, I remember, the Lord of Hosts was there, and he knows how to marshal armies. But how was it that they were willing to sit in groups? People are not always so willing to be ordered about, and when they are hungry they are often very disobedient; but they sat down as they were told to do, and sat down in groups, so that they were divided with little aisles between them. The original word, used by Mark, represents them as divided like beds of flowers, with walks between, so that as a gardener can go up and down and water all the plants, so the waiters at the feast could conveniently give every man his share of bread and his piece of fish without confusion. *They sat down in groups of hundreds and of fifties.* Things do not look so orderly now, do they, as we see Christ, through his church, feeding the multitudes?

There is a good work going on in the north of England; there is a revival in Scotland; there is an awakening in Ireland; there is a stir in the midland counties; but does it not look very much like a scramble? Do we not seem to tumble over one another instead of doing our work in soldierly order? A good work springs up in one place all of a sudden, while religion is dying out in other quarters; the people are satisfied yonder, and are starving only a little way off. We do not get at the masses as a whole, or see the church progress in all places. Let us not, however, judge too hastily, for Jesus makes *his* order out of *our* disorder. We see a piece of the puzzle, but when the whole shall be put together, and we shall see the end from the beginning, I warrant you we shall see that Christ's great feast of mercy, with its myriads of guests, has been conducted on a principle of order as mathematically accurate as that which guides the spheres in their courses. God has laid down in the book of his everlasting purposes, written by him of old, everything that shall occur in the great economy of his grace, and from that he never swerves. His purposes ripen at the proper time, and his plans are carried out according to the wisest method.

Providence, which so often looks wild and blustering, is not so by any means; it is working in harmony with grace for the salvation of as many as Christ has bought with his most precious blood, and for the accomplishment of the grand intentions of electing love. The raising up of this minister and of that, the building of this house of prayer and that, and even the bringing of a certain number of people at one time to listen, and the bringing of such and such persons rather than others, and the moving of the preacher's heart to speak in this manner and not in that, and to dwell upon that subject and not upon the other – all these things are so ordered that when the story of the Lord's great grace-banquet shall be told, we shall say to ourselves, "It could not have been better. He has done all things well." While we shall have to admire the grandeur of the works of grace as seen in the number of the saved, we shall also admire the orderliness of it in the way in which these saved ones were separated to Jesus by the right means, at the right time, and in the right place, in such a way as to bring the utmost possible glory to God.

I like to think this over sometimes, not that we may quiet ourselves when we do not see numbers saved, nor that we may ever grow indifferent to the great multitudes who remain unconverted; but that we may rest assured that our God is not disappointed, that his plans are not frustrated, and that, after all, the gospel is not preached in vain. You must not think, dear brother, because for a little while you have been preaching the gospel apparently without success, that there will be a deficit somewhere in God's account at the end of the chapter. You must not dream that because in certain countries the gospel light burns dimly, God is foiled and defeated.

> When the book of God's purposes shall be unfolded in history, there will be found no mistakes or blunders there.

When the book of God's purposes shall be all unfolded in actual history there will be found no blots, mistakes, or blunders there. He knows the end from the beginning, and his purposes shall be fulfilled in every jot and tittle, and in nothing shall the glory of God be marred. Though Satan may be laughing now, and every now and then the men of the world may boast against the people of God, it shall not be so in the close of the affair; but it shall be said of the entire matter that it was a grand banquet of mercy, and it was ordered well, and Christ, the great head of the house, made a divine display of his bountiful mercy in causing the multitude to taste of his grace. Our duty, I believe, is to urge the people to sit down and receive the Word; and the duty of the sinner is, especially when he comes to hear the gospel preached, to sit in the attitude of expectancy, desiring to obtain the blessing.

I like the thought of those people all sitting down, although I wonder if some of them did not say, "I shall not sit down. Feed me with two fish and five loaves? I could eat the whole. Feed all this multitude that way? I shall not sit down. Preposterous! Ridiculous!" One is surprised that somebody or other did not get up and say, "No, no, no, we are not to be deluded after this fashion. Show us the table, and show us something on it to sit down to, and then we will sit down, but not otherwise." Let us be always confident that when God inclines the people's hearts to come expecting a blessing and to wait upon him for it, it is then that the blessing comes. I could not imagine the five thousand sitting there waiting to be fed, and Christ not feeding them. Could you conceive of such a thing? Their sitting down in expectancy laid a sacred compulsion upon the divine compassion, to which it gladly yielded. Oh soul, if you sit down in your hunger before Christ, and say, "Lord, I know you can feed me, I expect you to feed me; by faith I open wide my mouth that I may eat of your flesh and drink of your blood," then assuredly you shall be fed. Never was such a soul sent away empty. If you believe in him so as to accept him, *you have him;* rejoice in him!

Enough, then, about the order of the feast.

And now a little about their food. They had bread and fish. Jesus seems to have made that his standing bill of provisions whenever he spread a banquet – bread and fish. They once gave *him* a piece of broiled fish, but he seems always to have given *them* bread and fish. Bread was enough, was it not? Yes, enough, but not enough for him to give, for he loves to supply a little more than enough. He would give a relish as well as a sufficiency: there was bread *and fish.* When Jesus Christ makes feasts for souls he gives them sufficiency – bread, all that they can want, all the necessities for their souls' life. Giving a sufficiency he also gives excellency: he gives fish, and there shall be savor and delight, and peace with God. You shall not say, "He has given me workhouse food: he doles out by half ounces exactly what I want, but he does not let me help myself to sweet morsels, or fat things full of marrow." No, you shall have more than you actually want; you shall find in your dish a secret something which will sweeten all, and many other precious things of which you shall sing, "He satisfies my mouth with good things."

Jesus might have called some of the people close to him and given them bread and fish, and then have fed the next group with bread only, but he did not do so. He gave bread and fish all around, and it is very sweet to think that all souls that come to Christ get the same spiritual food, and if they do not eat in the same measure it is their own fault, not his; for every promise that is in the Word of God is for every soul that believes in him, except where some promises are reserved for spiritual attainments, and then those spiritual attainments are to be sought after and may be reached by all the family. Oh, chief of sinners, if you come to Jesus, there is the same love in his heart for you as for the chief of saints. Oh, least, and weakest, and feeblest of all who believe in Jesus, there is the same covenant mercy and covenant blessing for you as for Paul or Peter. Bread and fish he gave to all who came to his table; and even so there is a uniformity of spiritual meat for all his brethren. Jesus is the same precious Christ to all his people.

What suitable food it was! Other kinds of food might have been either distasteful or indigestible to a considerable number, but bread and fish would surely suit all palates and all conditions. They might all be satisfied with such light and yet substantial food, and probably they all were so. And here was the beauty of it: they did all eat *and were filled*. It was the right food, and a most agreeable food; and there was so much of it that though they ate much, as I have no doubt they did, for they were very hungry, for they had been all day listening to sermons – and that is hungry work – still, for all that, there was enough for them, yes enough and to spare. Gospel provisions are adapted to all needs. Gospel provisions are plentiful, and are liberally given forth to all who come for them. Gospel provisions are sweet and pleasant to those who participate in them. Gospel provisions will satisfy the most eager appetites.

Come to this place, you hungry soul, you who have been to Moses, and from him obtained nothing but the stony law, come and eat the bread of heaven. Come, poor sinner, you who have been to the pleasures of sin and found nothing there but the husks that the swine eat, come to Jesus, and he will fill you to the full with a more divine meat.

THE MIRACLE OF THE LOAVES

But we must pass on, having noticed the guests, their order, and their food, to now notice the waiters.

The waiters at this feast were the disciples. Not the apostles, I think, merely, but the disciples – all of them. They each came and received a portion, and handed it around to the hundreds and the fifties. What a blessed thing it is that Jesus Christ has not taken upon himself to call all his people by his grace apart from instrumentality. He might have done so if he had chosen. The blessed Spirit does not stand in any need of us; it is his condescension which leads him to employ us. He might have sent the Bible into the world, and the only part we might have been permitted to take in it might have been the printing of it, the giving of it away or the selling of it, and there it might have been left. But instead of that he uses the living voice, the living example, and the faithful persuasions of his own revived disciples. And what an honor this is, what a privilege this is! I am sure I would have been very delighted that day to help to pass around the bread and the fish; would not you have been also?

> It is one of the greatest pleasures you can have in life to feed a hungry man.

It is one of the greatest pleasures you can have in life to feed a hungry man. If you have ever done it you will know that there is a look in his eyes, and a joy in the manner of his eating, which makes you whisper to others, "I wish you would come and see him eat." It gives you pleasure to see his pleasure. If he is very hungry, every mouthful is sweet to him, and you feel a sympathy with his gladness as his needs are supplied. What delightful work it must have been to serve out that bread and fish; but oh, to preach the gospel! To preach the gospel when God is blessing it to sinners!

I have just finished twenty-one years of preaching to this congregation, and they have been twenty-one years of toil, especially as the sermons have been printed every week, but I would not change the work for any conceivable occupation, or the happiness of preaching the gospel for any happiness except that of seeing Jesus face to face, and I really do not know that I wish for that till I am done preaching the gospel; for if souls are to be saved, I would far rather delay here to help in it than go to heaven itself. Oh, the joy it gives one to see men saved! Have I not seen them sometimes in the vestry, when I have talked with them and prayed with them, and they have risen from their knees and said, "I see it, sir; I understand it now. I never saw it before. I am a saved man. I believe in Jesus. I know he is my Savior."

If a man finds joy in having made ten thousand dollars in business, he may keep his joy; I would sooner have the bliss of winning one soul for Christ. There is an intense satisfaction in soul winning. These are the things George Herbert would have said, that make music in our bosoms when we lie awake at night. These are the things that make it sweet to live, and even sweet to die, if we may feed poor hungry souls with the bread of heaven. Now, I want all of you who love the Lord and have tasted of what he provides to busy yourselves with supplying others. I wish we had more young men coming forward to enter into Christian ministry, that more would devote their strength and talents to the preaching of the gospel. But, at the same time, we ought to have more persons busying themselves in the school, more talking about Jesus Christ in their various families, more friends who would open their rooms for prayer meetings, more who would in some way or other try to get at the hungry world with the gospel of Jesus Christ. "Well," says one, "but we must not push too much nor become intrusive." We do not find that any of the disciples labored under that fear. No one intrudes on a hungry man if he brings him bread to eat; and if the hungry man should be so unkind as to call it intrusion, I have no doubt that after he has been fed he will be very grieved with himself for having said so, and he whom he reproached will readily accept the apology.

Go and intrude yourselves, my brethren, among the hungry, with the bread of heaven; intrude yourselves between the living and the dead, as Aaron did with his smoking censer; intrude yourselves in the valley of dry bones, and cry aloud unto them, "Thus says the Lord, you dry bones, live"; intrude yourselves as Christ intruded into a world which despised and rejected him, to whom, after all, he is the only Savior.

We are getting on with our consideration of the miracle, for we have seen the food, and the waiters; now let us go a step farther, namely, to the blessing. There they sit all hungry, and the waiters are all ready; but our Lord will not proceed till he has worshiped and rendered thanks. There is something in his glance and gesture – he looked up to heaven.

What did that mean? "O Father, these loaves and fish are yours. You have given them to us. We thank you for them. And now, O Father, the power to make these sufficient for the emergency comes from heaven; grant it, we pray you." Brethren, always give that look upward before you begin your work. Say, "Lord, here am I, a poor nobody, trying to teach others and to bring souls to Christ. For what I am I thank you, for I am that by your grace; but if I am to be useful, you must make me so. Lord, I look up with the hope that you will look down."

After our Lord had looked up to heaven we find that he blessed and then he broke the loaves. Jesus must bless our labor or it will be fruitless. *He* could bless the bread for himself, but *we* must look away from ourselves for the blessing. May Jesus bless you all, and he will if you look up and say, "Lord, bless us." Always do that on Sabbath days especially, for those are great settled feasts of the Lord. Ask the Lord to bless what the preacher is going to say, and then it will be made profitable to you. After the blessing comes the distribution, but not till then. Oh, for more looking up to God, for in him lies our strength. Oh, for more praying; there can never be too much of that. If we stopped every evangelistic service for a while, and ceased from all teaching and preaching in order to spend a season in crying mightily unto the Lord, it might be the quickest way of doing the Lord's work. Pauses for prayer are not delays. Prayerless haste makes ill speed.

> **Pauses for prayer are not delays. Prayerless haste makes ill speed.**

Now came the work itself – the eating. The disciples distributed the bread and the fish as quickly as they could, and the people began to eat. They all ate of the provisions, and they were all filled. Now, what should every soul here conclude but this: if Jesus has provided spiritual meat, he has not provided it to be looked at. He has not set it before us that we may merely hear about it; he has provided it that it might all of it be eaten. What is there for me? Lord, I am hungry, grant me a meal. Oh souls, if you would hear sermons with the view of knowing what there is in them for yourselves, that you might feed upon them, what blessed work it would be to preach to you! But we hold up the bread of heaven, and sing about its excellencies, and tell you of its sweetness, and persuade you to taste and see how good it is; and then we have the unhappiness of seeing you turn your backs both upon it and upon the great Lord of the feast, and you go your way as if you cared neither for him nor for his generosities.

The disciples had not this sorrow to distress them. None of the multitude refused the Lord's provisions. The miracle of the loaves and fish would have been a poor, lame business if the crowds had not eaten of the food so wondrously supplied. What, Jesus Christ a Savior and no sinner saved? Christ a physician and no sick one healed? It would be a sorry business. We must have the sinners saved, and the sick ones healed, or Jesus is not honored. Ought not this to encourage all of you to lay hold upon Christ, because he is set forth on purpose to be laid hold upon? Ought not this to encourage you to feast upon him, because he must have been meant to be fed upon?

If you put two canaries in a cage tonight, and in the morning when they wake they see a quantity of seed in a box, what will the birds do? Will they stop and ask what the seeds are there for? No, but they each reason thus: "Here is a little hungry bird, and there is some seed; these two things go well together." And immediately they eat. Even thus, if you were in your right senses, and had not been perverted by sin, you would say, "Here is a Savior, and here is a sinner: these two things go well together. Dear Savior, save me, a sinner. Here is a feast of mercy, and here is a hungry sinner; what can that feast be for but for the hungry, and I am such. Lord, I will even apply myself to this blessed festival of yours; and unless you come and tell me to be gone, I will feast till I am full." Did you ever know Jesus to say to a sinner, "*You* have no right here"? No, but it is written, *"The one who comes to Me I will certainly not cast out."* No one was reprimanded for eating that day, or for eating too much, and neither will any sinner ever be blamed for taking hold upon Christ, or for taking too hearty a hold upon him.

Come and take him, O anxious one, and the more fully you can take him the more will Jesus be pleased. Why does the river flow but to make glad your fields? Why does the fountain sparkle but to quench your thirst? Why does the sun shine but for your eyes to be blessed with its light? As you breathe the air around you because you feel it must have been made for you to breathe, so receive the full, free salvation of Jesus Christ because it is provided, and you are in need of it. No mandate of heaven exists to shut you out, but every sacred doctrine is an argument as to why you should come, and welcome, and take Jesus freely. The crowds all ate; none were so obstinate as to decline the free provisions. Did they receive the bread which perishes? I charge you, then, accept gladly the bread which endures to life eternal.

Now, when they had all eaten, there came the clearing away. There must be a clearing up after every banquet. They went around and gathered up the fragments that remained, and found twelve baskets full. This, as has often been remarked, teaches us economy in everything that we do for God: not economy as to giving to him, but as to the use of the Lord's money. Break your alabaster boxes, and pour out the sacred nard with blessed wastefulness, for that very wastefulness is the sweetness of the gift; but when God entrusts you with any means to use for him, use those means with discretion. When we have money given to us for use in God's cause, we should be more careful with it than if it were our own; and the same rule applies to other matters.

When God gives ministers a good time in their studies, and they read the Word and it opens up before them, they should keep notes of what comes to them. The wind does not always blow in the same manner, and it is well to grind your wheat when the mill will work. You should put up your sails, and let your ship fly along when you have a good, favoring breeze, and this may make up for dead calms. Economically set aside the fragments that remain after you have fed next Sunday's congregation, so that there may be something for hard times when your head aches, and you are dull and heavy in pulpit preparations.

But I think the beauty of it was this, that after they had all been fed there was *something left*. Did I hear a heavy heart complain – "I heard of a great revival, and a great blessing, but I was not there; I had just gone out of the town when that blessing came. Woe is me, I am too late." Ah, there is plenty left. No repentant sinner is too late. Sometimes friends come in at the end of a meal, and there is nothing left beyond the bare bones, but here is quite enough for you. Here are twelve baskets full to the brim. You are not too late. Come and welcome. Peter, bring some of that bread and fish. You have a whole basketful, hand it out. Let this poor latecomer have his portion. What if the revival did miss you, and what if the Sabbath sermon did not bless you, though it blessed so many! Nevertheless, come along, there is something left.

And there is this to be remarked too, that there was *something left for the waiters*. The five thousand did all eat; but there were twelve apostles who managed the distribution, and they had a basketful each to themselves. That was more than they had when they began. They had each a basketful. Many a time we, who are the waiters upon you in the gospel feast, do not get as much as you do. I have sometimes on a Sabbath day likened myself to a butcher who is selling his meat: this person comes for a joint, and that customer carries away a round of beef, while a third has a sirloin; thus I have dealt out the meat of the gospel, while I have been very hungry myself. There seemed to be nothing for me but the chopper and the block. Is it not so occasionally with you teachers in your classes? Have you not found it so, you preachers in the street? You tread out the corn, but are as starved as muzzled oxen. It shall not always be so. Go on feeding the people, and you shall sit down afterwards; a great basketful will remain for you at the end.

I remember a good story of one of our young brethren from the college. He preached one Sabbath afternoon what he thought to himself was a dull, powerless sermon. He was going away very much discouraged, when an aged minister said to him, "My dear brother, there are two tokens that God can give you of your being called, and they are such as he gave to Gideon. He can make the fleece wet while all the barn floor around is dry; or he can reverse the token, and he can make all the ground wet while the fleece is dry. Now, which token would you like to have?" "Oh sir," said the young man, "I see what you are driving at. If I could but hope that all the people were wet this afternoon, I would not mind being dry myself." We may well choose, my brethren, to be dry fleeces if all our hearers are wet with the dew of heaven.

I like the sign best to come as a wet fleece and a wet barn floor too, and when the Lord gives that, it is a favor indeed. Such was the divine abundance in this case. He gave the food for the five thousand, and the twelve basketfuls for those who waited on them, so that not a grumbler went away, nor a latecomer had to say, "There was none for me," nor a waiter missed his share. Now, brethren, can you not believe that if fifty thousand men had come trooping up that hill just then, if every blade of grass on that mountain had suddenly turned into a man, and if from among the overgrown marshy land, and the heather, and the bushes, and the stones, a great multitude, such as that which shall gather on the judgment day, had all started up all of a sudden, and they had all come and sat around the Savior, he would have still stood there and multiplied the loaves and the fish right away, and continued giving to his disciples till everyone was filled.

Sure I am that if all London should come to Jesus they would find enough in him for them. If all my fellow countrymen, alas, and all the human race that dwells upon the face of the earth, should be moved to come crowding around the Savior, there would be no fear of exhausting his power to save. We should not even have to hesitate for a moment, but still stand and preach the gospel to every creature, and still using, in the power of the Holy Spirit, the same cry: *"He who has believed and has been baptized shall be saved."* Come then, weary, hungry sinner; you have nothing to do but to take Christ. You do not have to bake the bread or broil the fish. The bread and fish are broken, blessed, and ready. Open your mouth and enjoy the food. Faith to receive what Christ provides is all that is needed. Lord grant it. Take salvation freely. Freely Jesus gives it to you. Take it, and God bless you; and if you have never had Christ before, and you get him today, you will have a happy future, after the sort that we read of in the Bible, when *they began to celebrate.* Come, for all things are ready. Turn not away. God bless you, for Christ's sake. Amen.

> **Faith to receive what Christ provides is all that is needed.**

Chapter 11

Certain Curious Calculations about Loaves and Fish

"Do you not remember, when I broke the five loaves for the five thousand, how many baskets full of broken pieces you picked up?" They said to Him, "Twelve." "When I broke the seven for the four thousand, how many large baskets full of broken pieces did you pick up?" And they said to Him, "Seven." And He was saying to them, "Do you not yet understand?" (Mark 8:18-21)

The disciples had come on board the vessel and had forgotten to bring bread with them: good men's memories sometimes fail them. For that reason they were greatly disturbed in mind, and they supposed that Jesus was disturbed also, and that he had shaped his speech so as to give them an indirect rebuke when he mentioned the leaven of the Pharisees. How little they understood his mind, though they had been so long a time with him! His thoughts were not occupied with bread for himself; neither was there any burdensome care in his heart about bread for them. His mind was at perfect rest about all secular things; and even as to all spiritual things he was by no means tossed about. Notwithstanding all his trials and his sorrows, I suppose that there never was a more serene mind than that of Jesus Christ our Lord. His heart was as great as an ocean, and though visited with terrible tempests, yet was it the Pacific Ocean still. *They* might be troubled about bread, but *he* was resting about that and all things besides. The winds which tossed the little lakes of their little minds into boiling cauldrons did not suffice to create a ripple upon the surface of his mighty soul.

Is it not well for us at this hour that it is so? We are fluttered and dismayed, but the mind of our great Lord is fearless and undisturbed. He will not fail nor be discouraged. The child cries because the ship rolls, but his father at the helm smiles at the storm; and what a mercy it is for the child that the father can smile, for if the captain were weak, where would the vessel be? If the father's heart failed him, where would his boy look for comfort? Calm face of Jesus, we look up to you, and we are quieted!

The Master, wishing to comfort his servants, bid them to consider what they already knew, and review what they had already seen. Usually the eyes of the Christian should be directed forward. It is foolish to try to live on past experience; it is a very dangerous, if not a fatal habit to judge ourselves to be safe because of something that we felt or did twenty years ago. Yet, for all that, we may look back to gain practical lessons for times of service, and comfortable lessons for hours of trial. Like the archer, we may draw the string back that it may shoot the arrow onward with greater force.

The Master asks his followers whether they had used their eyes. *"Having eyes, do you not see?"* They had seen two wonderful miracles by which thousands of persons had been fed, but had they really seen them? Had they been satisfied just to look at the bread and the fish, and at the feasting multitude, and then to let the whole scene melt away from them? Had they really heard the voice of what the Lord had done? *"Having ears, do you not hear?"* Had they missed the message altogether? Then he adds, *"Do you not yet understand?"* Do you not know what my action meant when I multiplied the loaves? Do you not see how it reveals my all-sufficiency? Have you not spelled between the lines this word – that God feeds all things – that he opens his hand and supplies the need of every living thing? Have you not yet discovered by those two miracles that there is nothing impossible with your Lord?

May we not also have missed our Lord's meanings very often? May we not have walked through a palace of wonders without observing the gleams of glory, the flashes of light eternal? Our unbelief is the undeniable evidence that we have not learned all that we ought to have done, for the outcome of spiritually seeing, perceiving, and understanding is faith. He that believes little has learned little; he that doubts and is troubled is but a babe, needing still to learn the basic principles of holy scholarship.

The Lord further asks them that tender question, *"And do you not remember?"* Brethren, we remember much that we ought to forget, and we forget much that we ought to remember. Down the stream of memory floats refuse from the city of Sodom, and we diligently gather it; but down the same stream descends costly timber from Lebanon, and we permit it to drift by us. Our sieve holds the chaff and rejects the corn. It ought not to be so. Let us look back upon the whole of our past lives at this hour with a careful, leisurely glance, and see whether there is not enough in our diaries to condemn our doubts and bury our cares, or at least to shut up our anxieties in a cage made of the golden bars of past mercy, and fastened in with jeweled bolts of gratitude. *The Lord has been mindful of us; He will bless us.* Let us glory in what the Lord is going to do, and magnify his name for his mercy which is yet to be revealed. Let each one of us sing with David, *Then I will go to the altar of God, to God my exceeding joy; . . . I shall praise You, O God, my God.* Then has memory performed her part correctly, when from the altars of the past she has snatched a living coal with which to set on fire the incense of today.

> The outcome of spiritually seeing, perceiving, and understanding is faith.

Not being able to read your own personal diaries, for these are only known to yourselves, I shall endeavor to take you back to the records of the disciples' memories, and we will think of the text as it brings before us the two great miracles of feeding the hungry. May we learn from them what the Spirit intends to teach us by them.

And the first thing I shall want to bring to your recollection is the daring, yet unavoidable, project. This was the daring project – to feed five thousand persons in the wilderness. Two hundred pennyworth was the calculation of one of the ready reckoners of the hour. Some men are always very ready at counting the pennies which they have not gotten.

Whenever there is a holy deed to be done, our mathematically minded unbelievers are prompt with their estimates of cost and their prudent forecastings of grave deficiencies. We are great at calculations when we are little at believing. How can the necessary amount be raised? It is so much a head among so many members. Unfortunately, the heads do not yield the poll tax, and the money does not come, and confidence in man leaves us weeping by the broken cistern. This is the way in which a large part of the church's thought boils up, evaporates, and is wasted. Alas, for those calculations about pennyworths! Or else it is, *"Where will anyone be able to find enough bread here in this desolate place?"* From what source? as if there could be any "source" but one. Where does everything come from by which man lives? Does it not come from God? It goes round about in different channels, but it knows only one source. When any of the channels fail, the fountain is still flowing; and he that has faith to *go* to it directly shall not lack.

But it did seem to the disciples a very preposterous idea that with nothing but sand, and stone, and rock round about them, they would make a banquet for five thousand men. Is it not much more preposterous that the Christian church should have to evangelize such a city as London? It may not seem so to you, but if you lived in the midst of the extreme poverty of the East End, you would think it the problem of problems, how to reach the sunken multitudes. We little dream on what a volcano we live. The pent-up misery and the seething sin of London may yet produce a second edition of the French Revolution unless the grace of God shall intercede. The people are famishing bodily, mentally, morally, and spiritually, and we must feed them. I marvel not if in the presence of these dying millions you cry, "From where?" But then London is only one out of many cities. Our whole nation is a small fraction of the myriads of our race. China, India, Africa are yet to be fed. The command is, *"Go into all the world and preach the gospel to all creation."* The proposal is that the knowledge of the Lord shall yet cover the earth as the waters cover the sea, and I repeat the keynote which I sounded just now – it is a daring project: startling to the thoughtful, impossible to the calculating, hard even to the believing.

But then, you see, in the case of the disciples in the wilderness it was an inevitable project. However strange the proposition might seem, it pressed upon them; they could not avoid it, for the people had no provisions with them, and were fainting. Many of them had come from afar. If they attempted to go to their own homes without refreshment they would die by the way, and therefore it would not do to send the multitude away. They must be fed. "How is it to be done?" is the question, and whether they can answer it or not, the necessity is there all the same.

With the Savior it was an unavoidable necessity. *It would break his heart to see them fainting and famishing.* He could not endure it. At the very thought of their destitute condition he was moved with compassion. His whole nature was stirred, convulsed, and filled with excitement at the sight of hunger, paleness, weariness, and faintness. The great Shepherd *must* feed these hungry sheep. It is not a question with him, "Can it be done?" or "Can it not be done?" but it *must* be done. One of the imperial necessities which sometimes took possession of the royal heart of Christ had entered into his soul, and *he must* do its bidding. He himself took their infirmities and carried their sorrows. He was such an all-comprehending man that he included them within his own manhood. If they hungered, he hungered; if they fainted, he fainted; and if they died, he himself seemed to die; and, therefore, by the intense sympathy of his nature he was driven to feel that the multitude must be fed.

Just imagine that they had not been fed, that they had begun to faint and die of hunger all over those hills to which they had followed Jesus – *how it would have marred his ministry!* Why, surely, the disciples who had said somewhat cavalierly, *"Send the crowd away,"* would have been oppressed with a lifelong sorrow if their wish had been carried out. They never would have forgotten that dreadful dreary day, and the starvation, and the fainting, and the death which followed it. Think of what mischief it would have done to Christ's cause. The rumor that he led the people into solitary places, and that there they died of hunger would have been greatly derogatory to our Lord; for what prophet ever did this? What advantage the Pharisees would have made of it! How exultingly they would have cried, "Is this man after all a prophet like Moses, who fed the people with manna in the wilderness?" They would have cried, "He said that he was the Son of God; he claimed to have raised the dead; but if he had really possessed this power he would have fed the hungry multitude who had spent their strength in following him." No, the Christ cannot have it so. He has come to save men's lives; he cannot let them die. He must feed the crowd.

Now imagine, men and brethren, that we never carry out the commission which Christ has laid upon us today – that of teaching the multitude. Imagine that from this point on we never labor to win souls – that we give up London as a forlorn case, that we abandon the heathen world as assuredly given over to destruction, like a vessel driven by a hurricane upon an ironbound coast – imagine it, I say. Can you endure the imagination? I cannot abandon the drifting ship. Let us man the lifeboat! I know that some quiet themselves into a kind of despair as to the possibility of the Lord ever being king over this whole earth; will you try the wretched experiment? So these people must be left to die, for how can so many be fed? But the project of love shall be implemented; to that hope we cling, and to that end would we spend and be spent. If things look not so, and Christianity occupies as yet but a mere corner of the world, it matters not to our faith; we still believe. Faith counts no odds. One man with God on his side is in the majority if never another thinks as he does; therefore, in feebleness of numbers we are yet omnipotent in the might of the Most High.

> I am persuaded that the Lord has permitted the present sorrow so that he may produce from it a greater glory.

Had not the multitude been fed, *our Lord would have missed a grand occasion for the display of his grace.* Grace is sovereign, but it is abounding: wherever it finds suitable occasion, it displays its power. A hungering, fainting crowd! What space for compassion! What vantage ground for benevolence! It could not be that the Lord of love should let such an opportunity slip by; his love was too eager to display itself to lie quiet at such an hour. But, brethren, what an occasion for revealing the splendor of divine grace does the present age present! London is a brave canvas on which to paint a master picture of mercy, of power, of wisdom. What a block of marble the great world presents for the Infinite Sculptor! What a monument of grace will the human race become when it shall rejoice in God the Savior! I am persuaded that the Lord has permitted the present sorrow so that he may produce from it a greater glory. I am sure in my own soul that he permits the multitudes to hunger in this terrible wilderness simply and only that he may feed them, and thus prove to all the universe his power to bless.

I hope I have brought before your minds very clearly that amazing project which seemed most daring, and even preposterous, and yet was needful, and even inevitable.

Brethren, hoping for the help of God's good Spirit, I would take you, secondly, to another sight: the baffled disciples and their serene Master.

The Master had consulted Philip about supplies, in order that the difficulty of the case, and the insufficiency of mere means, might be seen by all. Philip found that all that was available was a lad's breakfast of five barley loaves and a few small fish; and he anxiously added, *"What are these for so many people?"* The prudent counselor had done his best, but it did not come to much. He left this problem unsolved: *"What are these for so many people?"* As for the rest of the disciples, they looked in Jesus' face with astonishment and blank despair, and said, *"Where would we get so many loaves in this desolate place to satisfy such a large crowd?"* But all the time that they were thus full of fidgets and worries, there stood the Master, calm as a sweet summer's evening, not in the least disturbed or troubled. What a difference between the feebleness and unbelief of the disciples and the mighty confidence of the Lord Jesus! How much need is there that we be changed from glory to glory as by the image of the Lord; for we also are very far as yet from being like him in our tone and spirit! We have not yet entered fully into his rest, nor shall we till we learn his faith in God.

Why was Jesus Christ, our Master, so calm? I have upon my mind the savor of a word the Lord once gave me for you upon that text: *He Himself knew what He was intending to do.* It is in great part our ignorance which puts us into such a quandary. We do not know what is going to be done; we are in suspense, and suspense eats into the soul as an acid eats into metal. "From what place? How? When? Where?" – all these questions prick us like so many daggers, and each prick kills a joy. "Our thoughts are all a case of knives," as George Herbert puts it, and every knife in that case destroys a hope. But the Master had no suspense; he knew what he would do. We shall get peace, brethren, when we also know what we should do. "Oh," say you, "I thought you were going to say when we know what *he* will do." Oh no! We probably will not know that till he does it. It is enough for us to know what *we* should do. "But," says one, "that is what we do *not* know." I answer, That is what we ought to know. We ought to know that we mean to leave everything with our Lord. If we once settled it in our minds that we would trust and not be afraid, what peace we would enjoy! If we will leave God's work with God, and simply trust, we shall drink into the peace of God.

Besides that, our Lord was thus calm because *he had faith, while they had nothing better than mere sense.* Here they were, as I have said before, counting the loaves and numbering the fish. Hear them saying, "Here are only five loaves, and they are of barley; and the fish are not only few, but small." They took care to record that fact, and to lay stress upon it; and they are equally clear as to the greatness of the hungry multitude, and the barrenness of the wilderness around them. They are all going on in that style, judging by the sight of the eyes and the touch of the hands; but the Son of God has another and better sense – he trusts his Father. Jesus, a man like themselves, has confidence that in the hour of his need the Godhead will not fail him, but will fulfill his needs. We have no Godhead in unity with our humanity; but yet we have more than Jesus had. "Oh," you say, "that cannot be!" You will admit my statement when I remind you that we have all that Christ had, and then we have Christ himself in addition. He has given us all that he has, so we have that; and then he has given us himself, so we possess the double. We ought never to doubt, but to rely upon the Godhead – Father, Son, and Holy Spirit – in every time of our necessity. *"In the mount of the Lord it will be provided";* Jehovah-Jireh: "The Lord Will Provide." Oh, for grace to cast all care away; to be baffled and worried no longer, but to rest and be still!

Moreover, one thing, I think, which made Christ so calm was that *he really acted while they only questioned.* He said, *"How many loaves do you have?" "Bring them here to Me."* He came at once to practical action. The people who do not believe in conversions are those who never convert anybody; but as soon as ever a man is led of the Spirit to turn men from darkness to light, and God blesses him in his work, he believes in it. He who has something to do has less temptation to doubt than the man who has nothing else to do but to doubt. Heresies in the Christian church never come from the city missionary, never from the faithful pastor, never from the intense evangelist, but always from gentlemen at ease, who take no actual part in our holy war. Those literary fools who criticize religion in reviews, and have nothing else to do except to put their hands to their heads and press whims out of their brows, these are the men that trouble us.

Our Lord Jesus Christ gave way to no sort of doubt, for he speedily took the bread and the fish in his hands, and began blessing and breaking them, while prompt upon his own action followed the divine energy which multiplied the little supply. If you and I would but serve the Lord in earnest, we might end our reckonings as to how much is to be done, and how it is to be done, and where it is to be done, and all that. Get to your work, my brother, and your doubts shall fly like chaff before the wind.

The baffled disciples, and the calm and quiet Master, make up an instructive picture; we shall have profited by it to the full if we also become calmly reliant upon God, and are no more carried away with unbelieving amazement.

Thirdly, and briefly, I want to set two more matters before your mind's eye for your comfort. In the miracles whereby we see the multitudes fed, we see the resources used, but we see Christ conspicuous.

You perceive that our Lord says of the loaves, *"Bring them here to Me."* The resources were used. When he has multiplied these very loaves and fish, he gives them to the men that are round about him, and of these the multitudes partake. Whatever men in their folly may say as to neglecting the outward resources, and sitting still and doing nothing because God will do his own work, we hear nothing of the kind from Jesus. He used the loaves, and he used the fish, and he used the men, though he could well enough have done without them. He was omnipotent and did not need them; but he was wise, and he would teach us the lesson that by instrumentality God's great work is to be done. Therefore, despise not resources, and at the same time do not rest in them.

But observe how the fish, and the loaves, and the men, and all the *resources were made to sink.* In that picture you see the great crowd. I do not think the painter needs to lay his colors on very vividly; he can draw the people as a kind of luminous haze if he likes. The one figure that stands out like the sun at noonday, hiding all else by the brilliance of his light, is the Master himself. Jesus only is glorious in that out-of-doors banqueting room. Where are those few fish? "Here," says one. "Here," cries another. "Here," shouts another. But those few and little fish cannot be in the hands of all those five thousand. Where has the bread gone to? "I have a loaf," cries one. "I have a loaf," says another, and they are all feeding as voraciously as they can. What has become of the original five loaves? Bring them here, brother, or at least go and make a diligent search for the original five loaves and those little fish, so that we may preserve one of them as a relic. What, can you not find one of them? You do not know where they are. They are all gone. Of course they are.

Whenever God blesses a man very greatly, that man sinks to nothing in his own esteem. If Peter's boat is full, Peter's boat sinks. If we are plunged in blessing up to the hilt, self is hidden under the weight of mercy. A little blessing, imagined to be something extraordinary, elevates the little man; but a great all-swamping blessing comes like a torrent, and bears the man and his littleness away, and nothing is seen but the Lord and the blessing. I am sure that it is so when the Lord uses any one of us as the means of doing good to others; we are humbled, and he is exalted.

> Whenever God blesses a man very greatly, that man sinks to nothing in his own esteem.

And after the miracle is over, when they go around to gather up the fragments in their twelve baskets or seven baskets, Peter has a quick eye, but ask him whether he can find one of those original loaves. He may go from basket to basket, and he cannot find one. It is lost in the creation which God has made out of it. And can he find in all those baskets the original fish? They must be there, for it is out of those fish that all the meat came to feed the people; but you cannot discover them. So it shall be if God will bless us, my brethren. People will gather around us and say, "What is there in this man? We perceive no supreme talent. What is there in this woman to make her so useful? We see nothing special about her." Never you mind. Let them pick at any bit of fish which they think they can see in your native talent or vigorous character; but as for yourself, you know that if any of the multitude are fed, the provision came from the Master's hand, when he took your little, and blessed and broke and multiplied it so as to make it suffice for the occasion. I believe that *resources are honored by Christ's using them,* but I am quite sure that before he is done with them the resources will sink into the uttermost obscurity, and Jesus Christ will be all in all, and that not because the resources are unblessed, but because they are blessed in so gracious a degree.

Furthermore, we see in the miracles of feeding, work accomplished of a marvelous kind, but power unexhausted. See those five thousand men and the women and the children! *They are all fed.* It is a proverb that there never was a feast but from which someone did not go away unsatisfied; but there is no rule without an exception. Here are two exceptions to that proverb. *They all ate and were satisfied* upon two occasions. It did not matter how many thousands there were, for not one of them was overlooked by the ever-blessed Host. It did not matter how hungry they were, for they all ate till they were full.

But this is the point I want to show you: *the power that multiplied the bread and fish, and fed the thousands, had not come to an end.* Their power to eat was exhausted, but not Christ's power to feed; for when they had received to their utmost capacity, there was still more to follow. The people were very hungry that day, the mountain air made their appetites keen, and their long fasting put a razor edge upon them; yet when they had all eaten to the full, great baskets were brought, and these were filled; in the one case twelve, and in the other case seven of them. There is enough for each, enough for all, and still enough remaining for future needs. The infinite Worker reveals his infinity by his unstinted bounty and his unmeasured liberality.

I cannot understand from the Greek what the size of these baskets may have been; the second set, the seven, have a name which shows that they were tolerably large, for Paul was let down in such a basket from the window when he escaped from his enemies in Damascus. The first sort which were used when there were twelve of them appear to me to have been larger still. They give you an idea of a coffin, or a coffer. They were large baskets of which it is said that men could sleep in them. Yet these baskets, whatever their size may have been, were filled – twelve and seven; and if the Lord had willed to do so, he could have filled twelve thousand baskets, or seventy thousand baskets. His power was running over; it could not be contained in earthly vessels, any more than a river can be held in a pitcher. It was still flowing in a copious stream when every mouth and every basket had been filled. Some seem to imagine that the Lord does everything by the inch and the ounce, keeping to limits and quantity; but this is rather the manner of men than the fashion of the Lord.

We know that the Lord Jesus Christ redeemed his elect from among men; therefore, some will have it that the merit of his atonement must be limited. No such thing. He gave himself for us, and there can be no measure to the value of such a gift. He died for our sins, and not for our sins only, but also for the sins of the whole world. His object was definite, but he achieved it by an agency which cannot be limited. He not only did that which he mainly aimed at, but he also did more, just as in this case he not only fed the thousands, but he also filled baskets with the fragments. The power of God, and the merit of the sacrifice of Christ, are among the infinite things; let us bow before the Lord, and rejoice in that which surpasses measure.

Moreover, brothers and sisters, whatever the Lord has given to you, he has still far more to bestow upon you. Whatever you may feast upon in this public service, there is yet a portion for you to take home with you in the basket and lay up in the storehouse. However God may have blessed you in your work for him in the past, he is still able to do exceedingly abundantly above all that you ask or even think. However much the church may have been increased by a true revival, God has never yet done according to the fullness of his ability in the church as yet; even Pentecost was but the firstfruits. I hear a voice from heaven saying, *"You will see greater things than these."* *"Greater works than these [you] will do; because I go to the Father."* We have been far from reaching the *ultima Thule* of sacred possibility. Still "the arrow is beyond you." We have never seen the best of our God as yet. We may go forward with the supreme faith that Pentecost has yet to be outdone – that all the mighty preachings of the fathers, when they turned nations to Christ, shall yet be exceeded in the triumphs of the cross in the latter days. We are approaching nobler ages, and God's great acts will not dwindle into trifles.

CERTAIN CURIOUS CALCULATIONS ABOUT LOAVES AND FISH

Remember that all that you could see, and all that you could know, would be but a minute portion of his glorious power. All that you could understand would only be a manifestation of the skirts of his garment. What omnipotence is, and especially what it is in the kingdom of grace, no one knows except God himself. Let us not limit the Holy One, nor bind the Infinite One. In our Father's house there is bread enough and to spare, even after millions have been satisfied from his supplies.

I am going to finish by observing that the details of these miracles were different, but they were equally instructive. Kindly listen to what I am now saying, not as to anything of remarkable weight, but still as to a matter of interest in which there may be more instruction than appears at first sight.

Concerning our Lord's great free dinners, mark, first, that *the remainder after the feast was greater than the stock when the banquet began.* They began with five loaves and two fish; they began on another occasion with seven loaves and a few fish; but they left off with twelve baskets full in the one case, and with seven baskets full in the other. Never was this done at any of your tables, I am sure, when your children have gathered for their meals. These people did all eat and were filled, and yet there was more left than when they began. This seems impossible, and yet it is the rule in the kingdom of grace. I have often found when I have come with a very small stock to feed you, brethren, that I have gone away with more than I came with. You have been refreshed, and I have been more full than when I handed out your portions to you. You have gone to the class, dear friend, and felt that you were scantily supplied for feeding your dear ones; but you have given them your all, and under the divine blessing there has been enough for the class, and a double portion for you. You went out with five loaves, and you came back with twelve baskets heaped up. Strange!

We may so give for God as to get in the giving, so spend as to increase in the spending, and so die for God as to live more than ever. If this be fact, what a wide field it opens to our hope, and how it banishes our fear! It shuts the door of the countinghouse where we calculate according to human reason, and it opens the doors of the treasury from where we may draw ever-growing supplies. Go, brother, and scatter your handful of seed, for you shall come again rejoicing, bringing sheaves with you! Give of your meal and oil to the Lord's servant, and your barrel and jar shall be replenished in the giving. Remember, Bunyan's rhyme is true spiritually as well as providentially:

> There was a man and some did count him mad,
> The more he gave away the more he had.

Next learn that *care is always taken by Christ of all the broken pieces.* The Lord All-sufficient is still the God of economy. Since Jesus could create as much food as ever he pleased, you might have thought that it was hardly worth his while to gather up the fragments; and yet he did so. Waste is of Satan, not of God. God is not lavish with creation, nor extravagant with miracles. Though the Lord can raise up in this place, if he pleases, fifty ministers in an instant, he may not do so; but what he would have us do is to make use of such powers as we have. If we are only fragments, our place is not on the ground, but in the basket. We must not allow ourselves to be thrown away, or to be consumed by an animal passion, or to be left to decay; but we must be in the Lord's storehouse, ready to be used when the time comes. We shall be of some use one of these days, if we are willing to be used.

If you, my friend, are not a whole loaf, you are a crust, and no crust may be wasted. If you are not a slice of bread, you are a crumb, and even crumbs are dear to hungry men. If you are not a big fish, still you may be a little fish, and you must not waste yourself, nor must the church of God allow you to be wasted, but use must be found for you somewhere. But what a wonderful thing this is – Omnipotence picking up crumbs! God All-sufficient, to whom the cattle on a thousand hills are as nothing – who could make a whole sea of fish, or ten thousand worlds of bread by his bare will, and nothing else; and yet he sets his disciples to gather up broken pieces so that nothing may be lost! Surely it severely becomes us to waste a penny, an hour, or an opportunity. Let us be severely economical for the Lord our God.

Notice a rather curious thing: *there was most left when there was least to begin with.* When they commenced the dinner with seven loaves, they gathered up seven baskets full, but when they had only five loaves, they filled twelve baskets with the fragments. I suppose the baskets to have been of the same size, for I do not discover that the second set of baskets was any larger than the first. However, from a stock of seven loaves, after all expenditure, there came seven baskets as a remainder; but when there were only five loaves, and a greater expenditure, there were twelve baskets full left for the waiters. This is peculiar. The more they begin with, the less they end with; and the less they begin with, the more they have when the feast is concluded. Yet I have often noticed that this does occur. Have not you noticed it?

When you and I have begun rather grandly, and God has blessed us, we have had great reason to thank him; but when we have begun very feebly, he has frequently blessed us far more, and we have ended by praising him upon the high-sounding cymbals. We have gone away wondering, "Five loaves and twelve baskets! Why, the other day, when I had seven loaves, I had only seven baskets!" Yes, let the rich rejoice when he is brought low, for he, like Job, shall be richer than before. Do not begin to sink in spirit because you seem to have declined in ability; but just be confident in God that in your case also there will be most reward at the end when there was least amount to work with.

> The more God blesses you, the less you shall see of any adequate reason in yourself why you should be blessed.

Note again that *there was less visible means when there was more done.* There were only five loaves, but they fed five thousand; when there were seven loaves, they fed only four thousand. The most was done when there was the least to do it with. And so it shall happen to you, O worker for Jesus; for the more God blesses you, the less you shall see of any adequate reason in yourself why you should be blessed. With your five loaves you shall feed your five thousand, while somebody who had seven shall do less than you.

Another curious thing is that *when there was most eaten there was most left.* When five thousand besides women and children ate as much as ever they could, they left more than the four thousand did. The smaller number could not eat so much as the greater, yet their remainder of food uneaten was less than when five thousand filled themselves to the full. It is a curious inversion of all our regulations. We suppose the larger our company, the less will remain. But here it seems that when the company was largest, then that which was left was largest; and when the company was smaller, then less was left. It is so with us: the more we have to draw from us spiritually, the more will remain for our own portion. We shall make no saving by reducing the number of those whom we serve, but rather the reverse.

One other thing also learn, and that is that *where there is the most work for Jesus there will be the most remuneration.* It is not so elsewhere, for men are often paid best for doing least; but in our Lord's case every man's reward shall be according to his service. Those who waited on the vast crowd of people could not get much to eat themselves during the meal, for they were fully occupied in handing the bread to others; but when all was over, the Master said to them, "So you have had a great company today, there were five thousand at the least. You must need refreshment yourselves; yonder are twelve baskets full of that which remains, divide them among yourselves." Another day their work was hard, but not quite so laborious. That extra thousand, that always brings in the excessive labor through overcrowding, had not been there, and they had supplied four thousand pretty pleasantly. Then it was that they received only seven baskets for their share: a liberal allowance, but still not so large as on the former occasion. If you will work for Christ, and give for Christ, and labor for Christ, you shall have a rich return of present joy from him, and this shall have a proportion in it.

Many people will always be poor because they never give to the cause of God. Poor people should give in order that they may not be poor any longer, and the rich should give in order that they may not become poor. I mean not that these are to be the chief motives, but they may have their place. You that have little ability should work hard with that little ability so that you may increase it; and you that have great ability of course should do so, because you have so many talents entrusted to you. The Lord will allow no service to remain unrecompensed; and work done for the poor and needy shall win its wage – not of debt, but of grace. Satan said, *"Does Job fear God for nothing?"* Suppose he had done so. The devil would have gone his way and said that God was a hard master, whose service brought no sort of reward with it. Either way, Satan would have made mischief, and as we have no wish to please him, we admit that we do not serve God for nothing, but that in keeping his commandments there is great reward. When the multitude are done feasting, your Master will let you sit down to dinner, and you shall have abundant joy with him.

The chief point for all of us is to get at the blessed work. In the name of the ever-living God, let us feed each one his man that is nearest to him till the whole company shall be fed; for the Christ is behind us, the Son of God is working with us. The bread is not our bread but his bread; and the feeding of the multitude is not our work, but his; and the power is not ours, but all his own, and to his name shall be all the glory. Amen.

Charles H. Spurgeon – A Brief Biography

Charles Haddon Spurgeon was born on June 19, 1834, in Kelvedon, Essex, England. He was one of seventeen children in his family (nine of whom died in infancy). His father and grandfather were Nonconformist ministers in England. Due to economic difficulties, eighteen-month-old Charles was sent to live with his grandfather, who helped teach Charles the ways of God. Later in life, Charles remembered looking at the pictures in *Pilgrim's Progress* and in *Foxe's Book of Martyrs* as a young boy.

Charles did not have much of a formal education and never went to college. He read much throughout his life though, especially books by Puritan authors.

Even with godly parents and grandparents, young Charles resisted giving in to God. It was not until he was fifteen years old that he was born again. He was on his way to his usual church, but when a heavy snowstorm prevented him from getting there, he turned in at a little Primitive Methodist chapel. Though there were only about fifteen people in attendance, the preacher spoke from Isaiah 45:22: *Look unto me, and be ye saved, all the ends of the earth.* Charles Spurgeon's eyes were opened and the Lord converted his soul.

He began attending a Baptist church and teaching Sunday school. He soon preached his first sermon, and then when he was sixteen years old, he became the pastor of a small Baptist church in Cambridge. The church soon grew to over four hundred people, and Charles Spurgeon, at the age of nineteen, moved on to become the pastor of the New Park Street Church in London. The church grew from a few hundred attenders to a few thousand. They built an addition to the church, but still needed more room to accommodate the congregation. The Metropolitan Tabernacle was built in London in 1861, seating more than 5,000 people. Pastor Spurgeon preached the simple message of the cross, and thereby attracted many people who wanted to hear God's Word preached in the power of the Holy Spirit.

On January 9, 1856, Charles married Susannah Thompson. They had twin boys, Charles and Thomas. Charles and Susannah loved each other deeply, even amidst the difficulties and troubles that they faced in life, including health problems. They helped each other spiritually, and often together read the writings of Jonathan Edwards, Richard Baxter, and other Puritan writers.

Charles Spurgeon was a friend of all Christians, but he stood firmly on the Scriptures, and it didn't please all who heard him. Spurgeon believed in and preached on the sovereignty of God, heaven and hell, repentance, revival, holiness, salvation through Jesus Christ alone, and the infallibility and necessity of the Word of God. He spoke against worldliness and hypocrisy among Christians, and against Roman Catholicism, ritualism, and modernism.

One of the biggest controversies in his life was known as the "Down-Grade Controversy." Charles Spurgeon believed that some pastors of his time were "down-grading" the faith by compromising with the world or the new ideas of the age. He said that some pastors were denying the inspiration of the Bible, salvation by faith alone, and the truth of the Bible in other areas, such as creation. Many pastors who believed what Spurgeon condemned were not happy about this, and Spurgeon eventually resigned from the Baptist Union.

Despite some difficulties, Spurgeon became known as the "Prince of Preachers." He opposed slavery, started a pastors' college, opened an orphanage, led in helping feed and clothe the poor, had a book fund for pastors who could not afford books, and more.

Charles Spurgeon remains one of the most published preachers in history. His sermons were printed each week (even in the newspapers), and then the sermons for the year were re-issued as a book at the end of the year. The first six volumes, from 1855-1860, are known as *The Park Street Pulpit*, while the next fifty-seven volumes, from 1861-1917 (his sermons continued to be published long after his death), are known as *The Metropolitan Tabernacle Pulpit*. He also oversaw a monthly magazine-type publication called *The Sword and the Trowel*, and Spurgeon wrote many books, including *Lectures to My Students, All of Grace, Around the Wicket Gate, Advice for Seekers, John Ploughman's Talks, The Soul Winner, Words of Counsel for Christian Workers, Cheque Book of the Bank of Faith, Morning and Evening*, his autobiography, and more, including some commentaries, such as his twenty-year study on the Psalms – *The Treasury of David*.

Charles Spurgeon often preached ten times a week, preaching to an estimated ten million people during his lifetime. He usually preached from only one page of notes, and often from just an outline. He read about six books each week. During his lifetime, he had read *The Pilgrim's Progress* through more than one hundred times. When he died, his personal library consisted of more than 12,000 books. However, the Bible always remained the most important book to him.

Spurgeon was able to do what he did in the power of God's Holy Spirit because he followed his own advice – he met with God every morning before meeting with others, and he continued in communion with God throughout the day.

Charles Spurgeon suffered from gout, rheumatism, and some depression, among other health problems. He often went to Menton, France, to recuperate and rest. He preached his final sermon at the Metropolitan Tabernacle on June 7, 1891, and died in France on January 31, 1892, at the age of fifty-seven. He was buried in Norwood Cemetery in London.

Charles Haddon Spurgeon lived a life devoted to God. His sermons and writings continue to influence Christians all over the world.

Other Similar Titles

***Life in Christ (Vol. 1 - 7),*
by Charles H. Spurgeon

Men who were led by the hand or groped their way along the wall to reach Jesus were touched by his finger and went home without a guide, rejoicing that Jesus Christ had opened their eyes. Jesus is still able to perform such miracles. And, with the power of the Holy Spirit, his Word will be expounded and we'll watch for the signs to follow, expecting to see them at once. Why shouldn't those who read this be blessed with the light of heaven? This is my heart's inmost desire.

– Charles H. Spurgeon

Available where books are sold.

Jesus Came to Save Sinners, **by Charles H. Spurgeon**

This is a heart-level conversation with you, the reader. Every excuse, reason, and roadblock for not coming to Christ is examined and duly dealt with. If you think you may be too bad, or if perhaps you really are bad and you sin either openly or behind closed doors, you will discover that life in Christ is for you too. You can reject the message of salvation by faith, or you can choose to live a life of sin after professing faith in Christ, but you cannot change the truth as it is, either for yourself or for others. As such, it behooves you and your family to embrace truth, claim it for your own, and be genuinely set free for now and eternity. Come and embrace this free gift of God, and live a victorious life for Him.

Available where books are sold.

**Words of Warning,
by Charles H. Spurgeon**

This book, *Words of Warning*, is an analysis of people and the gospel of Christ. Under inspiration of the Holy Spirit, Charles H. Spurgeon sheds light on the many ways people may refuse to come to Christ, but he also shines a brilliant light on how we can be saved. Unsaved or wavering individuals will be convicted, and if they allow it, they will be led to Christ. Sincere Christians will be happy and blessed as they consider the great salvation with which they have been saved.

Available where books are sold.

According to Promise,
by Charles H. Spurgeon

The first part of this book is meant to be a sieve to separate the chaff from the wheat. Use it on your own soul. It may be the most profitable and beneficial work you have ever done. He who looked into his accounts and found that his business was losing money was saved from bankruptcy.

The second part of this book examines God's promises to His children. The promises of God not only exceed all precedent, but they also exceed all imitation. No one has been able to compete with God in the language of liberality. The promises of God are as much above all other promises as the heavens are above the earth.

Available where books are sold.

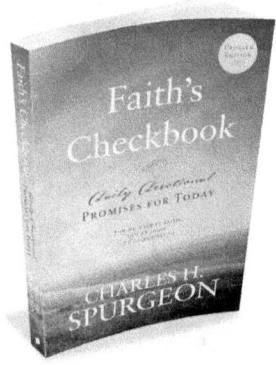

Faith's Checkbook, by Charles H. Spurgeon

Faith's Checkbook is a one-year devotional meant to encourage you to take God at His Word – to take hold of God's promises by faith. Each day you will be presented with a specific promise from the Bible, along with accompanying exhortation by Charles Spurgeon.

This is your "spiritual checkbook," if you will. God's bank account of provision is ample, and it cannot be overdrawn. Every situation you might face is equally met with a promise that, if accepted, will sufficiently see you through.

"God has given no promise that He will not redeem. He does not offer hope that He will not fulfill. To help my brethren believe this, I have prepared this little volume."
   – Charles H. Spurgeon

Available where books are sold.

Morning by Morning, **by Charles H. Spurgeon**

Charles H. Spurgeon's devotionals *Morning by Morning* and *Evening by Evening* have inspired, encouraged, and challenged Christians for generations. Spurgeon, with his masterful hand, carefully selected his text from throughout the Bible and covered a broad range of topics, in order to present a well-balanced and fruitful daily devotional for readers both young and old.

Now updated into more-modern English for today's readers, and again separated into two volumes as originally published, with morning devotionals in one volume and evening devotionals in the second. We chose a 11-point font for the sake of legibility, and formatted the devotionals so each fits on a single page.

Available where books are sold.

www.ingramcontent.com/pod-product-compliance
Lightning Source LLC
Chambersburg PA
CBHW070138080526
44586CB00015B/1745